I0148769

Oliver Goldsmith

She Stoops to conquer. A comedy in five Acts

2. Band

Oliver Goldsmith

She Stoops to conquer. A comedy in five Acts
2. Band

ISBN/EAN: 9783744789332

Printed in Europe, USA, Canada, Australia, Japan

Cover: Foto ©Thomas Meinert / pixelio.de

More available books at **www.hansebooks.com**

PRICE 15 CENTS.

DE WITT'S ACTING PLAYS.

(Number 203.)

S H E

STOOPS TO CONQUER.

A COMEDY, IN FIVE ACTS.

By OLIVER GOLDSMITH.

From the Author's approved Text as performed in the lead-
ing Theatres in Great Britain and the United States;
notably at Wallack's, New York, Feb. 25, 1876.

A thoroughly corrected and revised Acting Edition, giving
the text as the piece was originally performed at
Covent Garden, during the management of the
elder Colman, and under the direct
supervision of the Author.

AN ENTIRELY NEW EDITION.

TO WHICH ARE ADDED,

A Description of the Costumes—Cast of the Characters—Entrances and Exits—Relative Positions of the Performers on the Stage—Costumes—
Story of the Play—General Remarks—and the whole of
the Stage Business accurately marked.

New-York:

ROBERT M. DE WITT, PUBLISHER,

No. 33 Rose Street.

)W
LDF ☞ A COMPLETE DESCRIPTIVE CATALOGUE OF DE WITT'S ACTING
PLAYS, AND DE WITT'S ETHIOPIAN AND COMIC DRAMAS, containing
Plot, Costume, Scenery, Time of Representation, and every other informa-
tion, mailed free and post-paid.

DE WITT'S ETHIOPIAN & COMIC DRAMAS

Nothing so thorough and complete in the way of Ethiopian and Comic Dramas has been printed as those that appear in the following list. Not only are the plots, the characters droll, the incidents funny, the language humorous, but all the situations, positions, pantomimic business, scenery and tricks are so plainly set down, and explained, that the merest novice could put any of them on the stage. Included in them are all the most laughable and effective pieces of their class ever produced.

*** *In ordering, please copy the figures at the commencement of each play,* the number of the piece in "DE WITT'S ETHIOPIAN AND COMIC DRAMA." /

☞ *Any of the following Plays sent, postage free, on receipt of price—15 cents each*

Address, **ROBERT M. DE WITT,**

No. 33 Rose Street, New York.

☞ The figure following the name of the Play denotes the number of pages. The figures in the columns indicate the number of characters.—M. *male;* F. *female.*

*** Female characters are generally assumed by males in these plays.

[ST]OOPS TO CONQUER.

A Comedy,

IN FIVE ACTS.

OLIVER GOLDSMITH.

[AUTH]OR'S APPROVED TEXT AS PERFORMED AT THE
THEATRES IN GREAT BRITAIN AND THE
[UNIT]ED STATES; NOTABLY AT WALLACK'S,
NEW YORK, FEBRUARY 25, 1876.

CORRECTED AND REVISED ACTING EDITION, GIV-
[ING] AS THE PIECE WAS ORIGINALLY PERFORMED
[AT THE] GARDEN THEATRE, DURING THE MANAGE-
[MENT OF] THE ELDER COLMAN, AND UNDER THE DI-
[R]ECT SUPERVISION OF THE AUTHOR.

[E]NTIRELY NEW EDITION.

TO WHICH ARE ADDED,

[A DESCRIPTION OF] THE COSTUMES—CAST OF THE CHARACTERS—EN-
[TRANCES AND] EXITS—RELATIVE POSITIONS OF THE PERFORM-
[ERS ON TH]E STAGE—COSTUMES—STORY OF THE PLAY—
[CRITICA]L REMARKS—AND THE WHOLE OF THE
[STA]GE BUSINESS ACCURATELY MARKED.

NEW YORK:

[R]. M. DE WITT, PUBLISHER,

No. 33 ROSE STREET.

(BETWEEN DUANE AND FRANKFORT STREETS.)

COPYRIGHT, 1876, BY ROBERT M. DE WITT.

CAST OF CHARACTERS.

	Covent Garden, London, 1825.	Drury Lane, London, 1829.	Wallack's, N. Y., Feb. 25, 1876.	John st. Theatre, N. Y., Jan. 30, 1773.	Park Theatre, N. Y., Sept. 10, 1810.	Lafayette Theatre, N.Y., July 6, 1826.
Sir Charles Marlow	Mr. CHAPMAN.	Mr. W. BENNETT.	Mr. J. W. SHANNON.		Mr. DOYLE.	Mr. JONES.
Young Marlow	Mr. JONES.	Mr. JONES.	Mr. LESTER WALLACK.	Mr. HARPER.	Mr. SIMPSON.	Mr. BLAKE.
Hardcastle	Mr. FAWCETT.	Mr. W. FARREN.	Mr. JOHN GILBERT.	Mr. HENRY.	Mr. HOGG.	Mr. FISHER.
Tony Lumpkin	Mr. KEELY.	Mr. LISTON.	Mr. HARRY BECKETT.	Mr. HALLAM.	Mr. BRAY.	Mr. HYAT.
Hastings	Mr. DURUSET.	Mr. VINING.	Mr. C. A. STEVENSON.		Mr. CLAUDE.	Mr. BERNARD.
Stingo (Landlord)	Mr. ATKINS.	Mr. BEDFORD.	Mr. E. M. HOLLAND.		Mr. CLAUDE.	
Diggory	Mr. BARNES.	Mr. HUGHES.	Mr. W. J. LEONARD.		Mr. ROBERTSON.	
Simon	Mr. RYALS.	Mr. BRADY.				
Ralph	Mr. LEWIS.	Mr. EAST.	Mr. JOSEPHS.			
Roger	Mr. MEARS.	Mr. SHERIFF.	Mr. J. CURRAN.			
Mat Muggins	Mr. EVANS.	Mr. EATON.				
Tom Twist	Mr. BARNES.	Mr. BARNES.	Mr. C. E. EDWIN.			
Jack Slang	Mr. NORRIS.	Mr. YARNOLD.	Mr. F. MORGAN.			
Aminadab		Mr. WALSH.				
Jeremy	Mr. HEATH.	Mr. SALTER.				
Servant	Mr. HAYES.	Mr. HONNER.				
Miss Hardcastle	Miss FOOTE.	Miss MORDAUNT.	Miss ADA DYAS.	Mrs. HENRY.	Mrs. MASON.	Miss TILDEN.
Miss Neville	Miss JONES.	Mrs. NEWCOMBE.	Miss IONE BURKE.	Miss TUKE.	Miss CLAUDE.	Mrs. JONES.
Maid	Mrs. BOYLE.	Mrs. WEBSTER.	Miss ETHEL THORNTON.			
Mrs. Hardcastle	Mrs. DAVENPORT.	Mrs. C. JONES.	Madame PONISI.	Mrs. HAMILTON.	Mrs. HOGG.	Mrs. F. SHER.

TIME IN REPRESENTATION—TWO HOURS AND A HALF

SCENERY.

ACT I., *Scene* 1.—A room in Mr. HARDCASTLE's old mansion. [*Note.*—All the furniture and accessories in this house should be rich and substantial, but quiet and subdued in tone.]

Scene 2.—Large public room in "The Three Jolly Pigeons" Inn. R. and L. C. two large tables are set, with rude rush-bottomed chairs on each side, and one at head of each table. About R. 3 E. a very large old-fashioned fire-place, in which a wood fire is blazing. L. U. E. a small bar is arranged with a little counter and shelves.

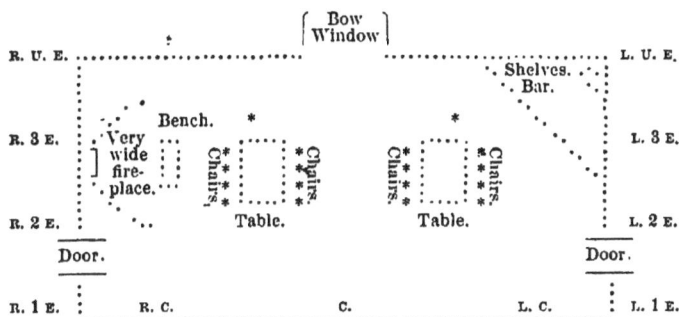

R. U. E. .... L. U. E.
                              ⌈ Bow ⌉
                              ⌊ Window ⌋
                                                          . Shelves. .
                                                           . Bar. .
                        Bench.   *   *
R. 3 E.   Very   L. 3 E.
           wide   Chairs.* *Chairs.   Chairs.* *Chairs.
           fire-
           place.
R. 2 E.   Table.   Table.   L. 2 E.

Door.   Door.

R. 1 E.   R. C.   C.   L. C.   L. 1 E.

ACTS II., III., and IV.—Parlor in Mr. HARDCASTLE's house. The fire-place is

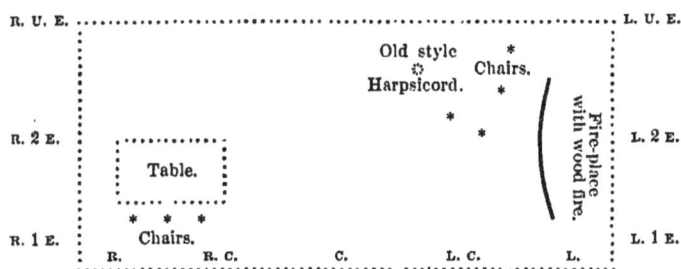

R. U. E. .... L. U. E.
                                        Old style   *
                                          ☼   Chairs.   *
                                        Harpsicord.   *
                                                    *
R. 2 E.   *   Fire-place L. 2 E.
                                                                 with wood fire.
           Table.
R. 1 E.   L. 1 E.
           * * *
           Chairs.
           R.   R. C.   C.   L. C.   L.

richly carved, but in old dark wood, all suggestive of solid comfort.

ACT V., *Scene I.*—Same as Act I., Scene 1.

Scene 2.—Garden and small park in rear of Mr. HARDCASTLE's mansion. L. C.

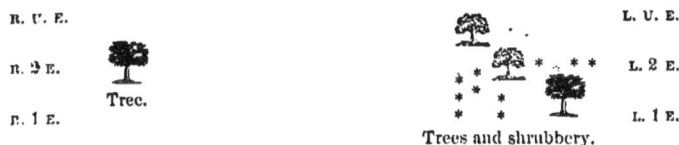

R. U. E.   L. U. E.

R. 2 E.   L. 2 E.
              Tree.
R. 1 E.   L. 1 E.
                                          Trees and shrubbery.

and L. **trees and ornamental shrubbery.** On R. C. 2 E. a tree, looking rudely like a man with arm extended, holding a pistol.

Scene 3.—Same as Act V., Scene 1.

COSTUMES.

Sir Charles Marlow.—Dark-blue breeches, and waistcoat; dark-blue camblet riding coat, with small cape; high black boots; three-cornered hat; powdered wig.

Mr. Hardcastle.—Dark plum-colored suit: knee breeches; dark silk stockings, and buckles in shoes; wig, yellowish.

Young Marlow.—Bottle-green surtout coat, with small cape; white waistcoat; close-fitting pantaloons, and very high black boots, mud-bespattered; three-cornered hat. *Second dress:* Mulberry-colored coat; white satin vest; lace cravat; fine white cassimere breeches; white silk stockings; black shoes, with diamond-mounted buckles.

Hastings.—Same dresses as Marlow, only varying in color of coats, and style of buckles.

Tony Lumpkin.—Scarlet hunting coat; black velvet jockey cap; white satin vest, elaborately and showily embroidered in colors; buckskin breeches, and top-boots. Tony carries a fox-hunter's whip with long lash, and should be an expert in its use. In Act V., Scene 2, Tony's boots should be spattered with mud.

Stingo.—Coarse cloth blue coat; corduroy breeches; blue yarn stockings; heavy shoes, and blue serge apron.

Diggory.—A plain, serviceable livery. His fellow servants in somewhat similar dress.

Mrs. Hardcastle.—*First dress:* Black quilted skirt, with overdress of heavy silk in extravagantly large flower patterns, tucked up in front, and gathered behind; silk stockings, and high heeled shoes, with paste buckles; head dressed in very high and extravagant style. *Second dress:* Plain stuff, dark petticoat, with mud on it; narrow, black cloak, and plain dark bonnet.

Miss Hardcastle.—*First dress:* Pale rose-colored lutestring silk dress, made and trimmed with taste and elegance. *Second dress:* Cherry spotted muslin gown; little white apron with pockets, trimmed with cherry-colored ribbon.

Miss Neville.—Blue silk waist; and white skirt, trimmed with narrow blue satin ribbon.

PROPERTIES.

Huntsman's whip for Tony; pipes (long clay); tobacco; bowl of punch and glasses for each table at "Three Pigeons;" a mallet for Tony; two candles in high, old style silver candlesticks; large silver tankard; bill of fare; jug of ale; jewel casket for Tony; prints on wall.

STAGE DIRECTIONS.

R. means Right of Stage, facing the Audience; L. Left; C. Centre; R. C. Right of Centre; L. C. Left of Centre. D. F. Door in the Flat, or Scene running across the back of the Stage; C. D. F. Centre Door in the Flat; R. D. F. Right Door in the Flat; L. D. F. Left Door in the Flat; R. D. Right Door; L. D. Left Door; 1 E. First Entrance; 2 E. Second Entrance; U. E. Upper Entrance; 1, 2 or 3 G. First, Second or Third Groove.

R.   R. C.   C.   L. C.   L.

☞ The reader is supposed to be upon the Stage, facing the Audience.

ing roles of this play. Space would not allow of our mentioning them all. So we come to the more recent revival of the piece (that which took place and was so finely rendered at "Walluck's" in the season of 1875-6). *Lester Wallack*, as YOUNG MARLOW, gave as fine a personation of this very difficult character as we have ever seen; he was equally good as the insolent fop, and the timid young gentleman; voice, facial expression, attitude, all were alike excellent. *Harry Beckett*, as TONY LUMPKIN, could have given almost any of his predecessors in the character "the long odds," and distanced the whole field. We doubt if ever the part of Mrs. HARD-CASTLE was entrusted to an abler representative than *Madame Ponisi*. The most exacting critic could find no flaw in this lady's admirable rendition of the fond, foolish, mother—so ridiculous and yet so natural. *Miss Dyas* made a pleasing Miss HARDCASTLE; but to those who remember *Mrs. Hoey* in the same character, it seemed by no means great. Miss NEVILLE was performed with an unobtrusive refinement and excellence characteristic of *Miss Ione Burke's* personations. *Mr. Gilbert*, as Mr. HARDCASTLE, has never played a character, to our thinking, in which he so completely filled all the requirements of the part. He looked, acted, and spoke, as if he had been really "to the *manor* born," and had often danced "Sir Roger de Coverly" at the head of his tenants. He looked indeed like a gentleman who might have dined with Johnson and have loaned Goldsmith a guinea. *Mr. E. M. Holland* was quite good in the stolid DIGGORY.

H. L. W.

PROLOGUE.

WRITTEN BY DAVID GARRICK.

Enter MR. WOODWARD, *dressed in black, and holding a handkerchief to his eyes.*

Excuse me, sirs, I pray, I can't yet speak,
I'm crying now—and have been all the week!
'Tis not alone this mourning suit, good masters;
I've that within—for which there are no plasters!
Pray would you know the reason why I'm crying?
The comic muse, long sick, is now a-dying!
And if she goes my tears will never stop;
For, as a play'r, I can't squeeze out one drop;
I am undone, that's all—shall lose my bread—
I'd rather, but that's nothing, lose my head.
When the sweet maid is laid upon the bier,
Shuter and *I* shall be chief mourners here.
To her a mawkish drab of spurious breed,
Who deals in sentimentals, will succeed!
Poor *Ned* and *I* are dead to all intents;
We can as soon speak Greek as sentiments!
Both nervous grown, to keep our spirits up,
We now and then take down a hearty cup.
What shall we do?—If comedy forsake us!
They'll turn us out and no one else will take us,
But why can't I be moral?—Let me try—
My heart thus pressing—fix'd my face and eye—
With a sententious look that nothing means
(Faces are blocks in sentimental scenes).
Thus I begin:—All is not gold that glitters;
Pleasure seems sweet, but proves a glass of bitters.
When Ign'rance enters Folly is at hand;
Learning is better far than house and land.
Let not your virtue trip, who trips may stumble;
And virtue is not virtue if she tumble.

I give it up—morals won't do for me ;
To make you laugh I must play tragedy.
One hope remains—hearing the maid was ill,
A doctor comes this night to show his skill.
To cheer her heart, and give your muscles motion,
He, in five draughts prepar'd, presents a potion ;
A kind of magic charm—for be assur'd
If you but swallow it the maid is cur'd ;
But desp'rate the doctor, and her case is,
If you reject the dose, and make wry faces !
This truth he boasts, will boast it while he lives,
No pois'nous drugs are mixed with what he gives.
Should he succeed you'll give him his degree ;
If not, within he will receive no fee !
The college, you must his pretensions back,
Pronounce him regular, or dub him quack.

EPILOGUE.

Well, having stooped to conquer with success,
And gain'd a husband, without aid from dress,
Still as a bar-maid I could wish it too,
As I have conquer'd him, to conquer you ;
And let me say for all your resolution,
That pretty bar-maids have done execution.
Our life is all a play, compo·ed to please,
" We have our exits and our entrances."
The first act shows the simple country maid,
Harmless and young, of everything afraid ;
Blushes when hir'd, and with unmeaning action,
" She hopes as how to give you satisfaction."
Her second act displays a livelier scene—
The unblushing bar-maid of a country inn ;
Who whisks about the house, at market caters,
Talks loud, coquets the guests, and scolds the waiters.
Next the scene shifts to town, and there she soars,
The chop-house toast of ogling connoisseurs ;
On 'squires and cits she there displays her arts,
And on the gridiron broils her lovers' hearts—
And as she smiles, her triumph to complete,
Even common councilmen forget to eat.
The fourth act shows her wedded to the 'squire,
And madam now begins to hold it higher ;
Pretends to taste, at operas cries *caro*,
And quits her Nancy Dawson for *Che Faro ;*
Doats upon dancing, and, in all her pride,
Swims round the room, the *Heinel* of Cheapside ;
Ogles and leers with artificial skill,
Till having lost in age the power to kill,
She sits all night at cards, and ogles at spadille.
Such through our lives the eventful history—
The fifth and last act still remains for me.
The bar-maid now for your protection prays,
Turns female barrister, and pleads for Bayes.

SHE STOOPS TO CONQUER.

ACT I.

SCENE I.—*A room in* Mr. Hardcastle's *old mansion.*

Enter Mrs. Hardcastle *and* Mr. Hardcastle, R.

Mrs. Hardcastle (c.). I vow, Mr. Hardcastle, you're very particular. Is there a creature in the whole country, but ourselves, that does not take a trip to town now and then, to rub off the rust a little? There's the two Miss Hoggs, and our neighbor Mrs. Grigsby, go to take a month's polishing every winter.

Mr. Hardcastle (R c.). Ay, and bring back vanity and affectation to last them a whole year. I wonder why London cannot keep its own fools at home? In my time, the follies of the town crept slowly among us, but now they travel faster than a stage-coach. Its fopperies come down, not only as inside passengers, but in the very basket.

Mrs. H. Ay, your times were fine times, indeed; you have been telling us of them for many a long year. Here we live in a rambling old mansion, that looks for all the world like an inn, but that we never see company. Our best visitors are old Mrs. Oldfish, the curate's wife, and little Cripplegate, the lame dancing-master; and all our entertainment your old stories of Prince Eugene and the Duke of Marlborough. I hate such old-fashioned trumpery.

Mr. H. And I love everything that's old; old friends, old times, old manners, old books, old wine; and I believe, Dorothy, (*tapping her under the chin*) you'll own I have been pretty fond of an old wife.

Mrs. H. Lord, Mr. Hardcastle, you're for ever at your Dorothy's, and your old wife's. You may be a Darby, but I'll be no Joan, I promise you I'm not so old as you'd make me by more than one good year. Add twenty to twenty, and make money of that.

Mr. H. (c.). Let me see! twenty added to twenty makes just fifty and seven.

Mrs. H. (L c.). It's false, Mr. Hardcastle; I was but twenty when I was brought to bed of Tony, that I had by Mr. Lumpkin, my first husband; and he's not come to years of discretion yet.

Mr. H. Nor ever will, I dare answer for him. Ay, you have taught him finely.

Mrs. H. No matter, Tony Lumpkin has a good fortune. My son is not to live by his learning I don't think a boy wants much learning to spend fifteen hundred a year.

Mr. H. Learning, quotha! a mere composition of tricks and mischief.

Mrs H Humor, my dear, nothing but humor. Come, Mr. Hardcastle, you must allow the boy a little humor.

Mr H. I'd sooner allow him a horsepond. If burning the footmen's
shoes frightening the maids, worrying the kittens, be humor, he has it.
It was but yesterday he fastened my wig to the back of my chair, and
when I went to make a bow, I popt my bald head in Mrs. Frizzle's
face.

Mrs. H. And am I to blame ? The poor boy was always too sickly
to do any good. A school would be his death. When he comes to be
a little stronger, who knows what a year or two's Latin may do for him ?

Mr H. Latin for him ! a cat and a fiddle ! No, no; the ale-house
and the stable are the only schools he'll ever go to.

Mrs. H Well, we must not snub the poor boy now, for I believe we
shan't have him long among us. Anybody who looks in his face may
see he's consumptive.

Mr H Ay, if growing too fat be one of the symptoms.

Mrs H. He coughs sometimes.

Mr. H. Yes, when his liquor goes the wrong way.

Mrs H I'm actually afraid of his lungs.

Mr. H. And tru'y so am I ; for he sometimes whoops like a speak-
ing-trumpet—(Tony *hallooing behind the scenes*, R.)—O, there he goes,
a very consumptive figure truly !

Enter Tony, R., *crossing to* L.

Mrs. H (L. c). Tony, where are you going, my charmer ? Won't
you give papa and I a little of your company, lovee ?

Tony (L.). I'm in haste, mother ; I can't stay !

Mrs. H. You shan't venture out this raw evening, my dear ; you
look most shockingly.

Tony. I can't stay, I tell you. The Three Pigeons expects me down
every moment. There's some fun going forward.

Mr. H. *aside* R.). Ay, the ale-house, the old place ; I thought so.

Mrs. H. A low, paltry set of fellows.

Tony. Not so low neither. There's Dick Muggins, the exciseman ;
Jack Slang, the horse-doctor ; Little Aminadab, that grinds the music-
box; and Tom Twist, that spins the pewter platter.

Mrs. H. Pray, my dear, disappoint them for one night, at least.

Tony. As for disappointing them, I should not so much mind; but I
can t abide to disappoint myself.

Mrs. H. L . *detaining him by seizing his whip, by which he drags
her about*). You shan't go !

Tony I will, I te'l you.

Mrs. H. I say you shan't !

Tony. We'll see which is the strongest, you or I.

[*Exit* L., *hauling her out.*

Mr. H. (c). Ay, there goes a pair, that only spoil each other. But
is not the whole age in a combination to drive sense and discretion out
of door ? There's my pretty darling Kate, the fashion of the times have
almost infected her too. By living a year or two in town, she is as fond
of gauze and French frippery as the best of them.

Enter Miss Hardcastle, R.

Blessings on my pretty innocence ! Drest out as usual, my Kate.
Goodness ! what a quantity of superfluous silk hast thou got about thee,

girl! I never could teach the fools of this age that the indigent world could be clothed out of the trimmings of the vain!

MISS HARDCASTLE (c.). You know our agreement, sir. You allow me the morning to receive and pay visits, and to dress in my own manner; and in the evening I put on my housewife's dress to please you.

MR. H. Well, remember I insist on the terms of our agreement; and by-the-bye, I believe I shall have occasion to try your obedience this very evening.

MISS H. I protest, sir; I don't comprehend your meaning.

MR. H. Then, to be plain with you, Kate, I expect the young gentleman I have chosen to be your husband from town this very day. I have his father's letter, in which he informs me his son is set out, and that he intends to follow him shortly after.

MISS H. Indeed! I wish I had known something of this before. Bless me, how shall I behave? It's a thousand to one I shan't like him; our meeting will be so formal, and so like a thing of business, that I shall find no room for friendship or esteem.

MR. H. Depend upon it, child, I'll never control your choice; but Mr. Marlow, whom I have pitched upon, is the son of Sir Charles Marlow, of whom you have heard me talk so often. The young gentleman has been bred a scholar, and is designed for an employment in the service of his country. I am told he's a man of an excellent understanding.

MISS H. Is he?

MR. H. Very generous.

MISS H. I believe I shall like him.

MR. H. Young and brave.

MISS H. I'm sure I shall like him.

MR. H. And very handsome.

MISS H. My dear papa, say no more. (*kissing his hand*) He's mine, I'll have him.

MR. H. And to crown all, Kate, he's one of the most bashful and reserved young fellows in all the world.

MISS H. Eh! you have frozen me to death again. That word reserved has undone all the rest of his accomplishments. A reserved lover, it is said, always makes a suspicious husband.

MR. H. On the contrary, modesty seldom resides in a breast that is not enriched with nobler virtues. It was the very feature in his character that first struck me.

MISS H. He must have more striking features to catch me, I promise you. However, if he be so young, so handsome, and so everything, as you mention, I believe he'll do still. I think I'll have him.

MR. H. Ay Kate, but there is still an obstacle. It is more than an even wager he may not have you.

MISS H. My dear papa, why will you mortify one so? Well, if he refuse, instead of breaking my heart at his indifference, I'll only break my glass for its flattery; set my cap to some newer fashion, and look out for some less difficult admirer.

MR. H. Bravely resolved! (*takes her hands*) In the meantime, I'll go prepare the servants for his reception; as we seldom see company, they want as much training as a company of recruits, the first day's muster.

[*Exit* L.]

MISS H. (c.). Lud! this news of papa's puts me all in a flutter! Young, handsome; these he put last; but I put them foremost. Sensible, good-natured; I like all that. But then reserved, and sheepish, that's much against him. Yet can't he be cured of his timidity by being taught to be proud of his wife? Yes, and can't I—But I vow I'm disposing of the husband before I have secured the lover.

Enter MISS NEVILLE, R.

I'm glad you've come, my dear. Tell me, Constance, how do I look
this evening? Is there anything whimsical about me? Is it one of
my well-looking days, child? Am I in face to-day?

MISS NEVILLE (c.). Perfectly, my dear. Yet now I look again—bless
me—sure no accident has happened among the canary birds or the gold
fishes? Has your brother or the cat been meddling? Or has the last
novel been too moving?

MISS H. No; nothing of all this. I have been threatened. I can
scarcely get it out—I have been threatened with a lover.

MISS N. And his name——

MISS H. Is Marlow.

MISS N. Indeed!

MISS H. The son of Sir Charles Marlow.

MISS N. As I live, the most intimate friend of Mr. Hastings, my admirer. They are never asunder—I believe you must have seen him
when we lived in town.

MISS H. Never.

MISS N. He's a very singular character, I assure you. Among women of reputation and virtue he is the modestest man alive; but his
acquaintance give him a very different character among creatures of
another stamp—you understand me.

MISS H. An odd character, indeed; I shall never be able to manage
him. What shall I do? Pshaw, think no more of him, but trust to
occurrences for success. But how goes on your own affair, my dear;
has my mother been courting you for my brother Tony, as usual?

MISS N. I have just come from one of our agreeable tête-à-têtes. She
has been saying a hundred tender things, and setting off her pretty
monster as the pink of perfection.

MISS H. And her partiality is such that she actually thinks him so.
A fortune like yours is no small temptation. Besides, as she has the sole
management of it, I'm not surprised to see her unwilling to let it go out
of the family.

MISS N. A fortune like mine, which chiefly consists in jewels, is no
such mighty temptation. But at any rate, if my dear Hastings be but
constant, I make no doubt to be too hard for her at last. However, I
let her suppose that I am in love with her son, and she never once
dreams that my affections are fixed upon another.

MISS H. My good brother holds out stoutly. I could almost love
him for hating you so.

MISS N. It is a good-natured creature at bottom, and I'm sure would
wish to see me married to anybody but himself. But my aunt's bell
rings for our afternoon's walk round the improvements. Allons! Courage is necessary, as our affairs are critical.

MISS H. Would it were bed-time, and all were well! [*Exeunt*, L.

SCENE II.—*Large public room in the "Three Pigeons" public house.*
R. C. *and* L. C., *two large tables are set, with rude, rush-bottomed
chairs on each side, and one at head of each table; about* R. 3 L.
L. *very large old-fashioned fire-place, in which a good wood-fire is
blazing;* L. U. E., *a small bar is arranged, with a little counter and
shelves* TONY *is seated at head of* R. C. *table, a little higher than
others. The other chairs are filled by rather shabby looking fellows.
All are supplied with long clay pipes, and glasses of punch.*

ALL. Hurrea! hurrea! hurrea! Bravo!

FIRST FELLOW, Now, gentlemen, silence for a song; the 'Squire is
going to knock himself down for a song.
ALL. Ay, a song! a song!
TONY. Then I'll sing you, gentlemen, a song I made upon this ale-
house, the Three Pigeons.*

> Let schoolmasters puzzle their brain,
>   With grammar, and nonsense, and learning,
> Good liquor, I stoutly maintain,
>   Gives genius a better discerning ;
> Let them brag of their heathenish gods,
>   Their Lethes, their Styxes, and Stygians;
> Their quis and their quæs, and their quods,
>   They're all but a parcel of pigeons,
>   Toroodle, toroodle, toroll.
>
> When old ranting preachers come down
>   A-preaching that drinking is sinful,
> I'll wager the rascals a crown,
>   They always preach best with a skinful:
> But when you come down with your pence,
>   For a slice of your scurvy religion.
> I'll leave it to all men of sense,
>   But you, my good friends, are the pigeons.
>   Toroodle, toroodle, toroll.
>
> Then come, put the jorum about,
>   And let us be merry and clever;
> Our hearts and our liquors are stout,
>   Here's the three jolly pigeons for ever;
> Let some cry up woodcock or hare,
>   Your bustards, your ducks, and your widgeons;
> But of all the birds in the air,
>   Here's a health to the three jolly pigeons!
>   Toroodle, toroodle, toroll.†

FIRST FEL. The 'Squire has got spunk in him.
SECOND FEL. I loves to hear him sing, bekeays he never gives us
nothing that's low.
THIRD FEL. O, d—n anything that's low, I can't a-bear it.
FOURTH FEL. The genteel thing is the genteel thing a'ter all. If so
be that a gentleman bees in a concatenation accordingly.
THIRD FEL. I like the maxim of it, Master Muggins. What though I
am obligated to dance a bear, a man may be a gentleman for all that.
May this be my poison, if my bear ever dances but to the very genteel-
est of tunes. Water Parted, or the Minuet in Ariadne.
SECOND FEL. What a pity it is the 'Squire is not come to his own! It
would be well for all the publicans within ten miles round of him.
TONY. Ecod, and so it would, Master Slang. I'd then show what it
was to keep choice of company.
THIRD FEL. O, he takes after his own father for that. To be sure,
old Squire Lumpkin was the finest gentleman I ever set my eyes on.
For winding the streight horn, or beating a thicket for a hare, or a
wench, he never had his fellow. It was a saying in the place, that he
kept the best horses, dogs, and girls, in the whole country.

---

* The song entitled "The Jolly Wagoners" was substituted for this, the author's, at "Wallack's."
† For the music of this song see last page.

Tony. Ecod! and when I'm of age I'll be no bastard, I promise you.
I have been thinking of Bet Bouncer and the miller's gray mare to begin with. But come, my boys, drink about and be merry, for you pay
no reckoning. Well, Stingo, what's the matter?

Enter Landlord, l.

Landlord (l.). There be two gentlemen in a post-chaise at the door.
They have lost their way upo' the forest; and they are talking something about Mr. Hardcastle.
Tony. As sure as can be, one of them must be the gentleman that's
coming down to court my sister. Then desire them to step this way,
and I'll set them right in a twinkling.   [*Exit* Landlord, l.
Gentlemen, as they mayn't be good enough company for you step down
for a moment, and I'll be with you in the squeezing of a lemon.
          [*Exeunt* Mob, r. 2 e.   Tony *rises and advances,* c.
Father-in-law has been calling me whelp, and hound, this half year.
Now if I pleased, I could be so revenged upon the old grumbletonian.
But then I'm afraid—afraid of what? I shall soon be worth fifteen hundred a year, and let him frighten me out of that if he can.

Enter Landlord, *conducting* Marlow *and* Hastings, l. Tony *goes
back.*

Marlow (l. c.) What a tedious, uncomfortable day have we had of
it? We were told it was but forty miles across the country, and we
have come above three-score.
Hastings (l. c —Tony *and* Stingo *confer at table in back ground*).
And all, Marlow, from that unaccountable reserve of yours, that would
not let us inquire more frequently on the way. (Tony *comes forward,*
r. c)
Mar. I own Hastings, I am unwilling to lay myself under an obligation to every one I meet, and often stand the chance of an unmannerly answer. .
Hast. At present, however, we are not likely to receive any answer.
Tony (*with his pipe in his hand,* r. c.). No offence, gentlemen. But
I'm told you have been inquiring for one Mr. Hardcastle, in these parts.
Do you know what part of the country you are in?
Hast. Not in the least sir; but should thank you for information.
Tony. Nor the way you came?
Hast. No, sir; but if you can inform us——
Tony. Why, gentlemen, if you know neither the road you are going,
nor where you are, nor the road you came, the first thing I have to inform you is, that you have lost your way.
Mar. We wanted no information of that, sir.
Tony. Pray, gentlemen, may I be so bold as to ask the place from
whence you came?
Mar. That's not necessary towards directing us where we are to go.
Tony. No offence; but question for question is all fair, you know.
Pray, gentlemen, is not this same Hardcastle a cross-grained, old-fashioned, whimsical fellow, with an ugly face; a daughter, and a pretty
son?
Hast. We have not seen the gentleman, but he has the family you
mention.
Tony. The daughter, a tall, trapesing, trolloping, talkative maypole.
The son, a pretty, well-bred, agreeable youth, that everybody is fond
of.

MAR. Our information differs in this. The daughter is said to be well-bred and beautiful; the son, an awkward booby, reared up, and spoiled at his mother's apron string.

TONY. He-he-hem! Then gentlemen, all I have to tell you is, that you won't reach Mr. Hardcastle's house this night I believe.

HAST. Unfortunate!

TONY. It's a d—d long, dark, boggy, dirty, dangerous way. Stingo, tell the gentlemen the way to Mr. Hardcastle's—(*winking upon the* LANDLORD) Mr. Hardcastle, of Quagmire Marsh, you know. (*returns to the table—lights his pipe—stands tittering.*)

LAND. (R. C.). Master Hardcastle's! Lack-a-daisy, my masters, you're come a deadly deal wrong! When you came to the bottom of the hill you should have crossed down Squash Lane.

MAR. Cross down Squash Lane?

LAND. Then you were to keep straight forward, till you came to where four roads meet.

MAR. Come to where four roads meet?

TONY (*comes from* L. *to* C.). Ay; but you must be sure to take only one of them.

MAR O sir, you're facetious.

TONY. Then keeping to the right, you are to go sideways till you come upon Crackskull Common; there you must look sharp for the track of the wheel, and go forward till you come to Farmer Murrain's barn; coming to the Farmer's barn, you are to turn to the right and then to the left, and then to the right about again, till you find out the old mill——

MAR. Zounds, man! we could as soon find out the longitude!

HAST. What's to be done, Marlow?

MAR This house promises but a poor reception; though perhaps the landlord can accommodate us.

LAND. (R.). Alack, master; we have but one spare bed in the whole house.

TONY. And to my knowledge, that's taken up by three lodgers already. (*after a pause, in which the rest seem disconcerted*) I have hit it. Don't you think Stingo, our landlady could accommodate the gentlemen by the fireside, with—three chairs and a bolster?

HAST. D—n your fireside!

MAR. (C.). And your three chairs and a bolster, say I.

TONY. You do, do you?—then let me see—what—if you go on a mile farther, to the Buck's Head? the old Buck's Head on the hill, one of the best inns in the whole country?

HAST. O ho! so we have escaped an adventure for this night, however.

LAND. (*apart to* TONY, R.). Sure, you ben't sending them to your father's as an inn, be you?

TONY (*apart to* STINGO). Mum, you fool you! Let them find that out. (*to them*) You have only to keep on straight forward, till you come to a large old house by the roadside. You'll see a pair of large horns over the door—that's the sign. Drive up the yard, and call stoutly about you.

HAST. Sir, we are obliged to you. The servants can't miss the way.

TONY. No no; but I tell you though, the landlord is rich, and going to leave off business; so he wants to be thought a gentleman, saving your presence, he! he! he! He'll be for giving you his company, and, ecod! if you mind him, he'll persuade you that his mother was an alderman, and his aunt a justice of peace.

LAND. A troublesome old ·blade, to be sure; but a keeps as good wines and beds as any in the whole country.

MAR. (L. C.). Well, if he supplies us with these, we shall want no further connection. We are to turn to the right, did you say?

TONY (L. C.). No, no; straight forward. I'll just step myself and show you a piece of the way. (*to the* LANDLORD, L.) Mum!

LAND. (L. C.). Ah, bless your heart, for a sweet, pleasant—d—d mischievous son of a——

[*Exeunt,* L. LANDLORD *skipping, as* TONY *cuts at him with his whip.*

CURTAIN.

ACT II.

SCENE I.—*Parlor in* MR. HARDCASTLE'S *house. The fire-place is richly carved, but in old dark wood, all suggestive of solid comfort.*

Enter HARDCASTLE, *followed by* DIGGORY *and three or four awkward* SERVANTS, L. 2 E.

MR. H. Well, I hope you're perfect in the table exercise I have been teaching you these three days. You all know your posts and your places, and can show that you have been used to good company, without stirring from home?

ALL (R. *and* L.). Ay! ay!

MR. H. When company comes, you are not to pop out and stare, and then run in again, like frightened rabbits in a warren.

ALL. No! no!

MR. H. You, Diggory, whom I have taken from the barn, are to make a show at the side table; and you, Roger, whom I have advanced from the plough, are to place yourself behind my chair. But you're not to stand so, with your hands in your pockets. Take your hands from your pockets, Roger; and from your head, you blockhead you! See how Diggory carries his hands. They're a little too stiff, indeed, but that's no great matter.

DIGGORY. Ay, mind how I hold them. I learned to hold my hands this way, when I was upon drill for the militia. And so being upon drill——

MR. H. You must not be so talkative, Diggory; you must be all attention to the guests. You must hear us talk, and not think of talking; you must see us drink, and not think of drinking; you must see us eat, and not think of eating.

DIG. By the laws, your worship, that's perfectly unpossible. Whenever Diggory sees yeating going forwards, ecod, he's always wishing for a mouthful himself!

MR. H. Blockhead! is not a bellyful in the kitchen as good as a bellyful in the parlor? Stay your stomach with that reflection.

DIG. Ecod, I thank your worship; I'll make a shift to stay my stomach with a slice of cold beef in the pantry.

MR. H. Diggory, you are too talkative. Then if I happen to say a good thing, or tell a good story, at table, you must not all burst out a-laughing, as if you made part of the company.

DIG. Then, ecod, your worship must not tell the story of old Grouse in the gunroom; I can't help laughing at that—he, he, he!—for the

soul of me. We have laughed at that these twenty years—ha, ha, ha!
(*all laugh.*)

MR. H. Ha, ha, ha! The story is a good one. Well, honest Diggory,
you may laugh at that—but still remember to be attentive. Suppose
one of the company should call for a glass of wine, how will you behave? A glass of wine, sir, if you please. (*to* DIGGORY) Eh, why don't
you move?

DIG. Ecod, your worship, I never have courage till I see the eatables
and drinkables brought upon the table, and then I am as bauld as a
lion.

MR. H. What, will nobody move?

FIRST SERV. I'm not to leave this place.

SECOND SERV. I'm sure it's no pleace of mine.

THIRD SERV. Nor mine, for sartin.

MR. H. You numskulls! and so while, like your betters, you are
quarrelling for place, the guests must be starved? O, you dunces! I
find I must begin all over again. (*bell rings*, L.) But don't I hear a
coach drive into the yard? To your posts, you blockheads! I'll go.
in the meantime, and give my old friend's son a hearty welcome at the
gate.   [*Exit*, L.

DIG. Zounds! my place is gone clean out of my head.

FIRST SERV. Where the devil is mine?

SECOND SERV. My place is to be nowhere at all; so I'ze go about my
business. [*Exeunt* SERVANTS, *running about frightened, different ways.*

Enter SERVANTS, *with candles, showing in* MARLOW *and* HASTINGS, L.

SERV. Welcome, gentlemen, very welcome. This way.

HAST. After the disappointments of the day, welcome once more,
Charles, to the comforts of a clean room, and a good fire. Upon my
word, a very well-looking house; antique, but creditable.

MAR. The usual fate of a large mansion. Having first ruined the
master by good housekeeping, it at last comes to levy contributions as
an inn.

HAST. As you say, we passengers are to be taxed to pay all these
fineries. I have often seen a good side-board, or a marble chimney-
piece, though not actually put in the bill, inflame the bill confoundedly.

MAR. Travellers, George, must pay in all places. The only difference
is, that in good inns you pay dearly for luxuries; in bad inns you are
fleeced and starved.

HAST. You have lived pretty much among them. In truth I have
been often surprised that you, who have seen so much of the world,
with your natural good sense, and your many opportunities, could
never yet acquire a requisite share of assurance.

MAR. The Englishman's malady. But tell me, George, where could
I have learned that assurance you talk of? My life has been chiefly
spent in a college, or an inn, in seclusion from that lovely part of the
creation that chiefly teach men confidence. I don't know that I was
ever familiarly acquainted with a single modest woman—except my
mother. But among females of another class you know——

HAST. Ay, among them you are impudent enough of all conscience.

MAR. They are with us, you know.

HAST. But in the company of women of reputation I never saw such
an idiot, such a trembler; you look for all the world as if you wanted
an opportunity of stealing out of the room.

MAR. (C). Why, man, that's because I do want to steal out of the
room. Faith, I have often formed a resolution to break the ice, and

rattle away at any rate. But I don't know how, a single glance from a pair of fine eyes has totally overset my resolution. An impudent fellow may counterfeit modesty, but I'll be hanged if a modest man can ever counterfeit impudence.

Hast. (r. c.). If you could but say half the fine things to them that I have heard you lavish upon the bar-maid of an inn, or even a college bed-maker.

Mar. Why, George, I can't say fine things to them. They freeze, they petrify me. They may ta'k of a comet, or a burning mountain, or some such bagatelle; but to me a modest woman, drest out in all her finery, is the most tremendous object of the whole creation.

Hast. Ha! ha! ha! At this rate, man, how can you ever expect to marry?

Mar. Never, unless, as among kings and princes, my bride were to be courted by proxy. If, indeed, like an Eastern bridegroom one we e to be introduced to a wife he never saw before, it might be endured. But to go through all the terrors of a formal courtship, together with the episode of aunts, grandmothers, and cousins, and at last to blurt out the broad staring question of " Madam, will you marry me ?" No, no, that's a strain much above me, I assure you.

Hast. I pity you. But how do you intend behaving to the lady you are come down to visit at the request of your father ?

Mar. As I behave to all other ladies. Bow very low, answer "yes," or "no," to all her demands. But for the rest, I don't think I shall venture to look in her face till I see my father's again.

Hast. I'm surprised that one who is so warm a friend can be so cool a lover.

Mar. To be explicit, my dear Hastings, my chief inducement down was to be instrumental in forwarding your happiness, not my own. Miss Neville loves you ; the family don't know you ; as my friend you are sure of a reception, and let honor do the rest.

Hast. My dear Marlow ! But I'll suppress the emotion. Were I a wretch, meanly seeking to carry off a fortune, you shou'd be the last man in the world I would apply to for assistance. But Miss Neville's person is all I ask, and that is mine, both from her deceased father's consent, and her own inclination.

Mar. Happy man ! You have talents and art to captivate any woman. I'm doomed to adore the sex and yet to converse with the only part of it I despise. This stammer in my address, and this awkward prepossessing visage of mine, can never permit me to soar above the reach of a milliner's 'prentice, or one of the duchesses of Drury Lane. Pshaw ! this fellow here to interrupt us !

Enter HARDCASTLE, L.

Mr. H. (l. c.). Gentlemen, once more you are heartily welcome. Which is Mr. Marlow ? Sir, you're heartily welcome. It's not my way, you see, to receive my friends with my back to the fire. I like to give them a hearty reception in the old style at my gate. I like to see their horses and trunks taken care of.

Mar. (*aside*). He has got our names from the servants already. (*to* Hardcastle) We approve your caution and hospitality. (*to* Hastings) I have been thinking, George, of changing our travelling dresses in the morning, I am grown confoundedly ashamed of mine.

Mr. H. (*putting chairs and tables in order in background*) I beg, Mr. Marlow, you'll use no ceremony in this house.

HAST. I fancy, George, you're right; the first blow is half the battle. I intend opening the campaign with the white and gold.

MR. H. (*still busy in background*). Mr. Marlow—Mr. Hastings—gentlemen—pray be under no restraint in this house. This is Liberty Hall, gentlemen. You may do just as you please here.

MAR. Yet, George, if we open the campaign too fiercely at first, we may want ammunition before it is over. I think to reserve the embroidery to secure a retreat

MR. H. (*puts a chair between them and sits*). Your talking of a retreat, Mr. Marlow, puts me in mind of the Duke of Marlborough, when he went to besiege Denain. He first summoned the garrison——

MAR. (*sits, R. c*). Aye, and we'll summon your garrison, old boy.

MR. H. He first summoned the garrison, which might consist of about five thousand men——

HAST. (*sits, L. c*). What a strange fellow is this!

MR. H. I say, gentlemen, as I was telling you, he summoned the garrison, which might consist of about five thousand men——

MAR. Well, but suppose——

MR. H. Which might consist of about five thousand men, well appointed with stores, ammunition, and other implements of war. Now, says the Duke of Marlborough to George Brooks, that stood next to him—you must have heard of George Brooks—I'll pawn my dukedom, says he, but I take that garrison without spilling a drop of blood. So——

MAR. What, my good friend, if you give us a glass of punch in the meantime, it would help us to carry on the siege with vigor.

MR. H. Punch, sir?

MAR. Yes, sir, punch. A glass of warm punch, after our journey, will be comfortable. This is Liberty Hall, you know.

MR. H. (*rises, and goes L.*). Here's a cup, sir.

MAR. (*aside*). So this fellow, in his Liberty Hall, will only let us have just what he pleases.

MR. H. (*taking the cup and drinks*). I hope you'll find it to your mind. I have prepared it with my own hands, and I believe you'll own the ingredients are tolerable. Will you be so good as to pledge me, sir? Here, Mr. Marlow. here is to our better acquaintance. (*drinks.*)

MAR. (*aside*). A very impudent fellow, this! but he's a character, and I'll humor him a little. (*aloud*) Sir, my service to you. (*drinks.*)

HAST. (*aside*). I see this fellow wants to give us his company, and forgets that he's an inn-keeper before he has learned to be a gentleman.

MAR. From the excellence of your cup, my old friend, I suppose you have a good deal of business in this part of the country. Warm work, now and then, at elections, I suppose?

MR. H. No, sir; I have long given that work over.

HAST. So, then, you have no turn for politics, I find?

MR. H. Why, no, sir; there was a time, indeed. when I fretted myself about the mistakes of government, like other people; but finding myself every day grow more angry, and the government no better, I left it to mend itself. Sir, my service to you. (*drinks.*)

HAST. So that, with eating above stairs, and drinking below, with receiving your friends within, amusing them without, you lead a good, pleasant, bustling life af it.

MR. H. I do stir about a great deal, that's certain. Half the differences of the parish are adjusted in this very parlor.

MAR. (*after drinking*). And you have an argument in your cup, old gentleman, better than any in Westminster Hall.

Mr. H. Aye, young gentleman, that, and a little philosophy.

MAR. (*aside*). Well, this is the first time I ever heard of an inn-keeper's philosophy.

HAST. So, then, like an experienced general, you attack them on every quarter. If you find their reason manageable you attack it with your philosophy; if you find they have no reason, you attack them with this. Here's your health, my philosopher. (*drinks.*)

MR. H. Good, very good, thank you; ha! ha! Your generalship puts me in mind of Prince Eugene, when he fought the Turks at the battle of Belgrade. You shall hear.

MAR. Instead of the battle of Belgrade, I think it's almost time to talk about supper. What has your philosophy got in the house for supper?

MR. H. For supper, sir? (*rises—aside*) Was ever such a request made to a man in his own house?

MAR. Yes, sir, supper, sir; I begin to feel an appetite. I shall make devilish work to-night in the larder, I promise you. (*pushes* HARDCAS-TLE *away, and lays his legs in his chair.*)

MR. H. (*stands amazed*, L. C. *Aside*). Such a brazen dog sure never my eyes beheld. (*to* MARLOW) Why, really, sir, as for supper, I can't well tell. My Dorothy and the cook-maid settle these things between them. I leave these kind of things entirely to them.

MAR. You do, do you?

MR. H. Entirely. By-the-bye, I believe they are in actual consultation upon what's for supper this moment in the kitchen.

MAR. Then I beg they'll admit me as one of their privy council. It's a way I have got. When I travel, I always choose to regulate my own supper. Let the cook be called. No offence, I hope, sir.

MR. H. O, no, sir, none in the least; yet I don't know how; our Bridget, the cook-maid, is not very communicative upon these occasions. Should we send for her she might scold us all out of the house.

HAST. Let's see the list of the larder, then. I ask it as a favor. I always match my appetite to my bill of fare.

MAR. (*to* HARDCASTLE, *who looks at them with surprise*). Sir, he's very right, and it's my way too.

MR. H. Sir, you have a right to command here. Here, Roger, bring us the bill of fare for to-night's supper—I believe it's drawn out. Your manner, Mr. Hastings, puts me in mind of my uncle, Colonel Gunthorp. It was a saying of his, that no man was sure of his supper till he had eaten it.

Enter ROGER, *with a bill of fare*, L.

HAST. (*aside*). All upon the high ropes! His uncle a colonel—we shall soon hear of his mother being a justice of the peace. But let's hear the bill of fare. [*Exit* ROGER, L

MAR. (*perusing*). What's here? For the first course, for the second course, for the dessert! The devil, sir! do you think we have brought down the whole joiner's company, or the corporation of Bedford? two or three little things, clean and comfortable, will do.

HAST. But let's hear it.

MAR (*reading*). "For the first course at the top, a pig's face and prune sauce."

HAST. D—n your pig, I say.

MAR. D—n your prune sauce, say I.

MR. H. And yet, gentleman, to men that are hungry, pig, with prune sauce, is very good eating But, gentlemen, you are my guests, make

what alterations you please. Is there anything else you wish to re-
trench or alter, gentlemen?

MAR. Why, really, sir, your bill of fare is so exquisite, that any one
part of it is full as good as another. Send us what you please. So
much for supper. And now to see that our beds are aired, and lug-
gage properly taken care of.

MR. H. I entreat you'll leave all that to me. You shall not stir a
step.

MAR. Leave that to you? I protest, sir. You must excuse me, I
always look to these things myself.

MR. H. I must insist, sir, you'll make yourself easy on that head.

MAR. You see I'm resolved on it. (*aside*) A very troublesome fellow
this, as ever I met with.

MR. H. Well, sir, I'm resolved at least to attend you. (*aside*) This
may be modern modesty, but I never saw anything look so like old-fashioned impudence.   [*Exeunt* MARLOW *and* HARDCASTLE, R.

HAST. So I find this fellow's civilities begin to grow troublesome.
But who can be angry at those assiduities which are meant to please
him? Ha! what do I see! Miss Neville, by all that's happy!

Enter MISS NEVILLE, L.

MISS N. (c.). Hastings! To what unexpected good fortune, to what
accident am I to ascribe this happy meeting?

HAST. Let me ask the same question, as I could never have hoped to
meet my dearest Constance at an inn.

MISS N. (L. C.). An inn? Sure you mistake! my aunt, my guardian,
lives here. What could induce you to think this house an inn?

HAST. My friend, Mr. Marlow, with whom I came down, and I, have
been sent here as to an inn, I assure you. A young fellow, whom we
accidentally met at a house hard by, directed us hither.

MISS N. Certainly it must be one of my hopeful cousin's tricks, of
whom you have heard me talk so often; ha! ha! ha! ha!

HAST. He whom your aunt intends for you? He of whom I have
such just apprehensions?

MISS N. You have nothing to fear from him, I assure you. You'd
adore him if you knew how heartily he despises me. My aunt knows it
too, and has undertaken to court me for him, and actually begins to
think she has made a conquest.

HAST. You must know, my Constance, I have just seized this happy
opportunity of my friend's visit here, to get admittance into the family.
The horses that carried us down are now fatigued with the journey,
but they'll soon be refreshed; and then, if my dearest girl will trust to
her faithful Hastings, we shall soon be out of their power.

MISS N. I have often told you, that though ready to obey you, I yet
should leave my little fortune behind with reluctance. The greatest
part of it was left me by my uncle, the India Director, and chiefly consists in jewels. I have been for some time persuading my aunt to let
me wear them. I fancy I'm very near succeeding. The instant they
are put into my possession, you shall find me ready to make them and
myself yours.

HAST. Perish the baubles! Your person is all I desire. In the meantime, my friend Marlow must not be let into his mistake. I know the
strange reserve of his temper is such, that if abruptly informed of it,
he would instantly quit the house, before our plan was ripe for execution.

MISS N. But how shall we keep him in the deception? Miss Hardcastle is just returned from walking: what if we persuade him she is come to this house as to an inn ?   Come this way. (*they confer.*)

Enter MARLOW, R.

MAR. (R.). The assiduities of these good people teaze me beyond bearing. My host seems to think it ill-manners to leave me alone. and so he claps not only himself but his old-fashioned wife on my back. They talk of coming to sup with us too, and then, I suppose, we are to run the gauntlet through all the rest of the family. What have we got here ?

HAST. My dear Charles ! Let me congratulate you—the most fortunate accident. What do you think is just alighted ?

MAR. Cannot guess.

HAST. (R. C.) Our mistresses. boy, Miss Hardcastle and Miss Neville. Give me 'eave to introduce Miss Constance Neville to your acquaintance. Happening to dine in the neighborhood, they called on their return to take fresh horses here. Miss Hardcastle has just stept into the next room, and will be back in an instant. Wasn't it lucky, he ?

MAR. (*aside*. I have just been mortified enough of all conscience, and here comes something to complete my embarrassment.

HAST. Well, but wasn't it the most fortunate thing in the world ?

MAR. O yes, very fortunate—a most joyful encounter! But our dresses George, you know, are in disorder. What if we should postpone the happiness till to-morrow—to-morrow at her own house. It will be every bit as convenient, and rather more respectful. To-morrow let it be. (*offering to go*, R., HASTINGS *stops him.*)

MI s N. (L. 1 E). By no means, sir. Your ceremony will displease her. The disorder of your dress will show the ardor of your impatience. Besides, she knows you are in the house, and will permit you to see her.

MAR. O, the devil she will! how shall I support it ? Hem! hem! Hastings. you must not go. You are to assist me, you know. I shall be confoundedly ridiculous !

HAST Pshaw, man! it's but the first plunge, all's over. She's but a woman. you know.

MAR. And of all women she that I most dread to encounter.

Enter MISS HARDCASTLE, *as returning from walking*, L.

HAST (C.., *introducing him*). Miss Hardcastle, Mr. Marlow. I'm proud of bringing two persons of such merit together, that only want to know, to esteem each other.

MISS H. (*aside*, L.) Now for meeting my modest gentleman. (*after a pause , during which* MARLOW *appears uneasy and disconcerted*) I'm glad of your safe arrival, sir—I'm told you had some accidents by the way.

MAR. (*embarrassed*). Only a few, madam. Yes, we had some. Yes, madam, a good many accidents, but should be sorry—madam—or rather glad of any accidents—that are so agreeably concluded. Hem !

HAST. (*to* MARLOW). You never spoke better in your whole life. Keep it up, and I'll insure you the victory.

MISS H. (L C.). I'm afraid you flatter, sir. You that have seen so much of the finest company can find little entertainment in an obscure corner of the country.

MAR. (*gathering courage*, L. C.). I have lived, indeed, in the world, madam; but I have kept very little company. I have been an observer upon life, madam, while others were enjoying it.

HAST. (*to* MARLOW). Cicero never spoke better. Once more, and you are confirmed in assurance for ever.

MAR (*to* HASTINGS). Hem! Stand by me then, and when I'm down, throw in a word or two to set me up again.

MISS H. An observer, like you, upon life, were, I fear, disagreeably employed, since you must have had much more to censure than to approve.

MAR. Pardon me, madam, I was always willing to be amused. The folly of most people is rather an object of mirth than uneasiness.

HAST. (*to* MARLOW). Bravo! bravo! never spoke so well in your whole life. Well, Miss Hardcastle, I see that you and Mr. Marlow are going to be very good company. I believe our being here will but embarrass the interview.

MAR. Not in the least, Mr. Hastings. We like your company of all things. (*to* HASTINGS) Zounds, George! Sure you won't go? How can you leave us?

HAST. Our presence will but spoil conversation, so we'll retire to the next room. (*to* MARLOW) You don't consider, man, that we are to manage a little tête-à-tête of our own.

[*Exeunt* HASTINGS *and* MISS NEVILLE, R.

MAR. (R., *aside*). What the devil shall I do? (*aloud*) Will you please to be seated, madam? (*gets a chair, and sets it by her,* L.) I say, ma'am—(*gets himself a chair, but sits in her chair.*)

MISS H Sir! (MARLOW *rises, and sits* R.)

MAR. I am afraid, ma'am, I am not so happy as to make myself agreeable to the ladies.

MISS H. (*sits,* L.). The ladies, I should hope, have employed some part of your addresses. (*she gradually removes her chair across to him.*)

MAR. (*relapsing into timidity*). Pardon me, madam—I—I—I—as yet have studied—only—to—deserve them.

MISS H And that, some say, is the very worst way to obtain them.

MAR. Perhaps so, madam. But I love to converse only with the more grave and sensible part of the sex. But I'm afraid I grow tiresome.

MISS H. Not at all, sir; there is nothing I like so much as grave conversation myself; I could hear it for ever. Indeed I have often been surprised how a man of sentiment could ever admire those light, airy pleasures, where nothing reaches the heart.

MAR. It's—a disease—of the mind, madam. In the variety of tastes there must be some who, wanting a relish—for—um—a—um—

MISS H. I understand you, sir. There must be some who, wanting a relish for refined pleasures, pretend to despise what they are incapable of tasting.

MAR. My meaning, madam, but infinitely better expressed.

MISS H. (*aside*). Who could ever suppose this gentleman impudent upon some occasions? (*to* MARLOW) You were going to observe, sir.

MAR. I was observing, madam—I protest, madam, I forget what I was going to observe.

MISS H (*aside*). I vow and so do I. (*to* MARLOW) You were observing, sir, that in this age of hypocrisy—something about hypocrisy, sir.

MAR Yes, madam. In this age of hypocrisy there are few who upon strict inquiry do not—a—a—a——

MISS H. I understand you perfectly.

MAR (*aside*). Egad! and that's more than I do myself.

MISS H. You mean that in this hypocritical age there are few who

do not condemn in public what they practise in private, and think they
pay every debt to virtue when they praise it.

Mar. True, madam; those who have most virtue in their mouths
have least of it in their bosoms. But I'm sure I tire you, madam.

Miss H. Not in the least, sir; there's something so agreeable and
spirited in your manner, such life and force. Pray, sir, go on.

Mar. Yes, madam, I was saying—But I see Miss Neville expecting
us in the next room. I would not intrude for the world.

Miss H. I protest, sir, I was never more agreeably entertained in all
my life.

Mar. (rises). But she beckons us to join her. Madam, shall I do
myself the honor to attend you?

Miss H. (rises). Well, then, I'll follow.   [Exit Marlow, R.

Ha, ha, ha, ha! Was there ever such a sober, sentimental interview?
I'm certain he scarce looked in my face the whole time. Yet the fellow, but for his unaccountable bashfulness, is pretty well too. He has
good sense, but then so buried in his fears that it fatigues one more
than ignorance. If I could teach him a little confidence it would be
doing somebody that I know a piece of service. But who is that somebody?—that, faith, is a question I can scarce answer.   [Exit, R.

Enter Tony, *with a jug of ale in his hand, and* Miss Neville, R.

Tony (R.). What do you follow me for, cousin Con? I wonder
you're not ashamed to be so very engaging.

Miss N. (R.). I hope, cousin, one may speak to one's own relations,
and not be to blame.

Tony (C.). Ay, but I know what sort of a relation you want to make
me though; but it won't do. I tell you, cousin Con, it won't do, so I
beg you'll keep your distance; I want no nearer relationship.
          [He runs off, L. 1 E., she follows.

Enter Mrs. Hardcastle *and* Hastings, R.

Mrs. H. (C.). Well, I vow, Mr. Hastings, you are very entertaining.
There's nothing in the world I like to talk of so much as London, and
the fashions, though I was never there myself.

Hast. (R. C.). Never there! You amaze me! From your air and
manner I concluded you had been bred all your life either at Ranelagh,
St. James's, or Tower Wharf.

Mrs. H. O, sir, you're only pleased to say so. We country persons
can have no manner at all. I'm in love with the town, and that serves
to raise me above some of our neighboring rustics; but who can have a
manner that has never seen the Pantheon, the Grotto Gardens, the
Borough, and such places where the nobility chiefly resort? All I can
do is to enjoy London at second-hand. I take care to know every
tête-à-tête from the Scandalous Magazine, and have all the fashions, as
they come out, in a letter from the two Miss Rickets of Crooked Lane.
Pray, how do you like this head, Mr. Hastings?

Hast. Extremely elegant and degagee, upon my word, madam. Your
friseur is a Frenchman, I suppose?

Mrs. H. I protest I dressed it myself from a print in the ladies' book
for the last year.

Hast. Indeed! Such a head in a side-box, at the playhouse, would
draw as many gazers as my Lady Mayoress, at a city ball.

Mrs. H. I vow, since inoculation began, there is no such thing to be seen as a plain woman; so one must dress a little particular, or one may escape in the crowd.

HAST. But that can never be your case, madam, in any dress. (*bowing.*)

MRS. H. Yet what signifies my dressing, when I have such a piece of antiquity by my side as Mr. Hardcastle? all I can say will not argue down a single button from his clothes. I have often wanted him to throw off his great flaxen wig, and, where he was bald, to plaster it over, like Captain Pately, with powder.

HAST. You are right, madam; for, as among the ladies, there are none ugly, so among the men, there are none old.

MRS. H. But what do you think his answer was? Why, with his usual gothic vivacity, he said, I only wanted him to throw off his wig to convert it into a tete for my own wearing.

HAST. Intolerable! At your age you may wear what you please, and it must become you.

MRS. H. Pray, Mr. Hastings, what do you take to be the most fashionable age about town?

HAST. Some time ago forty was all the mode; but I'm told the ladies intend to bring up fifty for the ensuing winter.

MRS. H. Seriously! Then I shall be too young for the fashion.

HAST. No lady begins now to put on jewels till she's past forty. For instance, miss there, in a polite circle, would be considered as a child, a mere maker of samplers.

MRS H. And yet my niece thinks herself as much a woman, and is as fond of jewels, as the oldest of us all.

Re-enter TONY *and* MISS NEVILLE. L. 1 E., *coquetting in the background.*

HAST. (R.). Your niece, is she? And that young gentleman, a brother of yours, I should presume?

MRS. H. (R.). My son, sir. They are contracted to each other. Observe their little sports. They quarrel and make it up again ten times a day, as if they were man and wife already. (*to them*) Well, Tony, child, what soft things are you saying to your cousin Constance this evening?

TONY (*advancing,* L. C.). I have been saying no soft things, but that it's very hard to be followed about so. Ecod! I've not a place in the house now that's left to myself but the stable.

MRS. H. Never mind him, Con, my dear. He's in another story behind your back.

MISS N. (L. C.). There's something generous in my cousin's manner. He falls out before faces to be forgiven in private.

TONY. That's a d—d confounded—crack!

MRS H. (L. C.). For shame, Tony. You a man, and behave so!

TONY (L.). If I'm a man, let me have my fortin'. Ecod! I'll not be made a fool of no longer.

MRS. H. Is this, ungrateful boy, all that I am to get for the pains I have taken in your education? Did not I work that waistcoat and those ruffles to make you look like a gentleman?

TONY. Ecod! I tell you I'll not be made a fool of no longer.

MRS. H. Wasn't it all for your good, viper? Wasn't it all for your good?

TONY. I wish you'd let me and my good alone then. Snubbing this way, when I'm in spirits. If I'm to have any good let it come of itself, not to keep dinging it, dinging it into one so. .

MRS. H. That's false! I never see you when you're in spirits. No, Tony, you then go to the ale-house or kennel. I'm never to be delighted with your agreeable wild notes, unfeeling monster.

TONY. Ecod! mamma, your own notes are the wildest of the two.

MRS. H. (*goes to* HASTINGS, R. C., *and pretends to weep*). Was ever the like! But I see he wants to break my heart, I see he does! (TONY *winks at* HASTINGS.)

HAST. Dear madam, permit me to lecture the young gentleman a little. I'm certain I can persuade him to his duty.

MRS. H. (L.). Well, I must retire. Come, Constance, my love. You see, Mr. Hastings, the wretchedness of my situation; was ever poor woman so plagued with a dear, sweet, pretty, provoking, undutiful boy?

[*Exeunt* MRS. HARDCASTLE *and* MISS NEVILLE, L.

TONY (C). Don't mind her, let her cry. It's the comfort of her heart. I have seen her and sister cry over a book for an hour together, and they said they liked the book the better the more it made them cry.

HAST. Then you're no friend to the ladies, I find, my pretty young gentleman?

TONY. That's as I find 'um.

HAST. Not to her of your mother's choosing, I dare answer? And yet she appears to be a pretty, well-tempered girl.

TONY. That's because you don't know her as well as I. Ecod! I know every inch about her; and there's not a more bitter, cantanckerous toad in all Christendom.

HAST. (*aside*). Pretty encouragement this for a lover.

TONY. I have seen her since the height of that. She has as many tricks as a hare in a thicket, or a colt in the first day's breaking.

HAST. To me she appears sensible and silent.

TONY. Ay, before company. But when she's with her playmates she's as loud as a hog in a gate.

HAST. Well, but you must allow her a little beauty. Yes, you must allow her some beauty.

TONY. Bandbox! She's all a made-up thing, mun. Ah, could you but see Bet Bouncer of these parts, you might then talk of beauty. Ecod! she has two eyes as black as sloes, and cheeks as broad and red as a pulpit cushion. She would make two of she.

HAST. Well, what say you to a friend that would take this bitter bargain off your hands?

TONY. Anon?

HAST. Would you thank him that would take Miss Neville, and leave you to happiness and your dear Betsy?

TONY. Ay, but where is there such a friend, for who would take her?

HAST. I am he. If you but assist me, I'll engage to whip her off to France, and you shall never hear more of her.

TONY. Assist you? Ecod! I will to the last drop of my blood. I'll clap a pair of horses to your chaise that shall trundle you off in a twinkling, and maybe get you part of her fortin' beside, in jewels, that you little dream of.

HAST. My dear 'Squire, this looks like a lad of spirit.

TONY. Come along then, and you shall see more of my spirit before you have done with me.   [*Exeunt*, L. TONY *singing*.

CURTAIN.

ACT III.

SCENE I —*Same as Scene I., Act II.*

Enter MR. HARDCASTLE, R.

MR. H. (c.). What could my old friend Sir Charles mean by recommending his son as the modestest young man in town? To me he appears the most impudent piece of brass that ever spoke with a tongue. He has taken possession of the easy-chair by the fireside already. He took off his boots in the parlor, and desired me to see them taken care of. I'm desirous to know how his impudence affects my daughter. She will certainly be shocked at it.

Enter MISS HARDCASTLE, *in second dress*, L.

Well, my Kate, I see you have changed your dress as I bid you; and yet, I believe, there was no great occasion.

MISS H. (c.). I find such a pleasure, sir, in obeying your commands, that I take care to observe them without ever debating their propriety.

MR. H. And yet, Kate, I sometimes give you some cause, particularly when I recommended my modest gentleman to you as a lover to-day.

MISS H. You taught me to expect something extraordinary, and I find the original exceeds the description.

MR. H. I was never so surprised in my life! He has quite confounded all my faculties!

MISS H. I never saw anything like it; and a man of the world too.

MR. H. Ay, he learned it all abroad. What a fool was I, to think a young man could learn modesty by travelling. He might as soon learn wit at a masquerade.

MISS H. It seems all natural to him.

MR. H. A good deal assisted by bad company and a French dancing-master.

MISS H. Sure you mistake, papa; a French dancing-master could never have taught him that timid look—that awkward address—that bashful manner——

MR. H. Whose look? whose manner, child?

MISS H. Mr Marlow's; his *mauvaise honte*, his timidity, struck me at the first sight.

MR. H. Then your first sight deceived you; for I think him one of the most brazen first-sights that ever astonished my senses.

MISS H. Sure, sir, you rally? I never saw any one so modest.

MR. H. And can you be serious! I never saw such a bouncing, swaggering puppy since I was born. Bully Dawson was but a fool to him.

MISS H. Surprising! He met me with a respectful bow, a stammering voice, and a look fixed on the ground.

MR. H. He met me with a loud voice, a lordly air, and a familiarity that froze me to death.

MISS H. He treated me with diffidence and respect; censured the manners of the age; admired the prudence of girls that never laughed; tired me with apologies for being tiresome; then left the room with a bow. and, Madam, I would not for all the world detain you. (*mimicking* MARLOW.)

MR. H. He spoke to me as if he knew me all his life before. Asked twenty questions, and never waited for an answer. Interrupted my best remarks with some silly pun; and when I was talking of the Duke of Marlborough and my friend Brooks, he asked if I had not a good hand at making punch. Yes, Kate, he asked your father if he was a maker of punch!

Miss H. One of us must certainly be mistaken.

Mr. H. In one thing, however, we are agreed—to reject him.

Miss H. Yes! But upon conditions. For if you should find him less impudent, and I more presuming; if you find him more respectful, and I more importunate—I don't know—the man is well enough for a man. Certainly he has a very passable complexion.

Mr. H. If we should find him so—but that's impossible. The first appearance has done my business; I'm seldom deceived in that.

Miss H. Then as one of us must be mistaken, what if we go to make further discoveries?

Mr. H. Agreed. But depend on't I'm in the right.

Miss H. And depend on't I'm not much in the wrong. [*Exeunt*, L.

Enter TONY, *running in with a casket*, R.

TONY. Ecod! I have got them. Here they are. My cousin Con's necklaces, bobs and all. My mother shan't cheat the poor souls out of their fortin' neither. O, my genus, is that you?

Enter HASTINGS, R.

HAST. My dear friend, how have you managed with your mother? I hope you have amused her with pretending love for your cousin, and that you are willing to be reconciled at last. We shall be ready to set off in a short time.

TONY. And here's something to bear your charges by the way. (*giving a casket*) Your sweetheart's jewels. Keep them, and hang those, I say, that would rob you of one of them.

HAST. But how have you procured them from your mother?

TONY. Ask me no questions and I'll tell you no fibs. I procured them by the rule of thumb. If I had not a key to every drawer in mother's bureau, how could I go to the ale-house so often as I do? An honest man may rob himself of his own at any time.

HAST. Thousands do it every day. But to be plain with you, Miss Neville is endeavoring to procure them from her aunt this very instant. If she succeeds, it will be the most delicate way at least of obtaining them.

TONY. Well, keep them till you know how it will be. But I know how it will be well enough; she'd as soon part with the only sound tooth in her head.

HAST. But I dread the effects of her resentment, when she finds she has lost them.

TONY. Never you mind her resentment, leave me to manage that. I don't value her resentment the bounce of a cracker. Zounds! here they are! Morrice—Prance! (*sits at a table near the flat,*)

[*Exit* HASTINGS, R.

Enter MRS. HARDCASTLE *and* MISS NEVILLE, R.

MRS. H. Indeed, Constance, you amaze me; such a girl as you want jewels! It will be time enough for jewels, my dear, twenty years hence, when your beauty begins to want repairs.

MISS N. (C.). But what will repair beauty at forty will certainly improve it at twenty, madam.

MRS. H. Yours, my dear, can admit of none. That natural blush is beyond a thousand ornaments. Besides, child, jewels are quite out at present. Don't you see half the ladies of our acquaintance, my Lady Kill-daylight, and Mrs. Crump and the rest of them, carry their jewels to town, and bring nothing but paste and marcasites back?

MISS N. But who knows, madam, but somebody that shall be nameless would like me best with all my little finery about me?

MRS. H. Consult your glass, my dear, and then see if, with such a pair of eyes, you want any better sparklers. (sees TONY) What do you think, Tony, my dear, does your cousin Con want any jewels, in your eyes, to set off her beauty?

TONY (rising). That's as hereafter may be.

MISS N. My dear aunt, if you knew how it would oblige me——

MRS. H. A parcel of old-fashioned rose and table cut things. They would make you look like the court of King Solomon at a puppet show. Besides, I believe I can't readily come at them. They may be missing for aught I know to the contrary.

TONY (L. C.—apart to MRS. HARDCASTLE). Then why don't you tell her so at once, as she's so longing for them? Tell her they're lost. It's the only way to quiet her. Say they are lost, and call me to bear witness.

MRS. H. (apart to TONY, L.). You know, my dear, I'm only keeping them for you. So, if I say they're gone, you'll bear me witness, will you? He! he! he!

TONY (goes R.). Never fear me. Ecod! I'll say I saw them taken out with my own eyes.

MISS N. (C.). I desire them but for a day, madam. Just to be permitted to show them as relics, and then they may be locked up again.

MRS. H (crosses to C.). To be plain with you, my dear Constance, if I could find them you should have them. They're missing, I assure you. Lost, for ought I know; but we must have patience wherever they are.

MISS N. I'll not believe it; this is but a shallow pretence to deny me. I know they're too valuable to be so slightly kept, and as you are to answer for the loss——

MRS. H. Don't be alarmed, Constance. If they be lost I must restore an equivalent. But my son knows they're missing, and not to be found.

TONY (goes back). That I can bear witness to. They're missing, and not to be found, I'll take my oath on't.

MRS. H. You must learn resignation, my dear; for though we lose our fortune, yet we should not lose our patience. See me, how calm I am.

MISS N. Ay, people are generally calm at the misfortunes of others.

MRS H. Now, I wonder a girl of your good sense should waste a thought upon such trumpery. We shall soon find them; and, in the meantime, you shall make use of my garnets till your jewels be found.

MISS N. (R.). I detest garnets. (TONY sits as before.)

MRS. H. The most becoming things in the world to set off a clear complexion. You have often seen how well they looked upon me. You shall have them.

MISS N. I dislike them of all things. You shan't stir. Was ever anything so provoking, to mislay my own jewels, and force me to wear trumpery!   [Exit MRS HARDCASTLE, R.

TONY (rises and runs to her). Don't be a fool. If she gives you the garnets, take what you can get. The jewels are your own already. I

have stolen them out of her bureau and she does not know it. Fly to
your spark—he'll tell you more of the matter. Leave me to manage
her.

Miss N. My dear cousin!

Tony. Vanish. She's here, and has missed them already. Zounds!
how she fidgets and spits about like a Catharine wheel!

[*Exit* Miss Neville, l.

Enter Mrs. Hardcastle, r., *screaming.*

Mrs. H. Confusion! thieves! robbers! We are cheated, plundered,
broke open, undone!

Tony (c.). What's the matter, what's the matter, mamma? I hope
nothing has happened to any of the good family!

Mrs H. We are robbed. My bureau has been broke open, the jewels
taken out, and I'm undone.

Tony. Oh, is that all? Ha! ha! ha! By the laws, I never saw it
better acted in my life. Ecod! I thought you was ruined in earnest.
Ha! ha! ha!

Mrs. H Why, boy, I am ruined in earnest. My bureau has been
broken open, and all taken away.

Tony. Stick to that; ha! ha! ha! stick to that; I'll bear witness,
you know; call me to bear witness.

Mrs. H. I tell you, Tony, by all that's precious, the jewels are gone,
and I shall be ruined forever.

Tony. Sure I know they are gone, and I'm to say so.

Mrs. H. My dearest Tony, but hear me. They're gone, I say.

Tony. By the laws, mamma, you make me for to laugh; ha! ha! ha!
I know who took them well enough; ha! ha! ha!

Mrs. H. Was there ever such a blockhead, that can't tell the difference between jest and earnest? I tell you I'm not in jest, booby.

Tony. That's right, that's right; you must be in a bitter passion, and
then nobody will suspect either of us. I'll bear witness that they are
gone.

Mrs. H. Was there ever such a cross-grained brute, that won't hear
me? Can you bear witness that you're no better than a fool? Was
ever poor woman so beset with fools on the one hand, and thieves on
the other?

Tony. I can bear witness to that.

Mrs H. Bear witness again, you blockhead you, and I'll turn you
out of the room directly. My poor niece, what will become of her?
Do you laugh, you unfeeling brute, as if you enjoyed my distress?

Tony. I can bear witness to that.

Mrs. H. Do you insult me, monster? I'll teach you to vex your
mother, I will. Here! thieves! thieves! thieves! thieves!

[*He runs off*, l 1 e., *she follows him.*

Enter Miss Hardcastle *and* Maid, l.

Miss H. (c.). What an unaccountable creature is that brother of
mine, to send them to the house as an inn; ha! ha! I don't wonder
at his impudence.

Maid (c.). But what is more, madam, the young gentleman, as you
passed by in your present dress, asked me if you were the bar-maid.
He mistook you for the bar-maid, madam.

Miss H. Did he? Then as I live I'm resolved to keep up the delusion. Tell me, Dolly, how do you like my present dress? Don't you think I look something like Cherry in the Beau's Stratagem?

MAID. It's the dress, madam, that every lady wears in the country, but when she visits or receives company.

MISS H. And are you sure he does not remember my face or person?

MAID. Certain of it

MISS H. I vow I thought so; for though we spoke for some time together, yet his fears were such that he never once looked up during the interview.

MAID. But what do you hope for from keeping him in his mistake?

MISS H. In the first place, I shall be seen, and that is no small advantage to a girl who brings her face to market. Then I shall perhaps make an acquaintance, and that's no small victory gained over one who never addresses any but the vilest of her sex. But my chief aim is to take my gentleman off his guard, and, like an invincible champion of romance, examine the giant's force before I offer to combat.

MAID. But are you sure you can act your part, and disguise your voice so that he may mistake that, as he has already mistaken your person?

MISS H. Never fear me. I think I have got the true bar cant—" Did your honor call?"—" Attend the Lion there "—' Pipes and tobacco for the Angel "—" The Lamb has been outrageous this half hour."

MAID. It will do, madam. But he's here.   [Exit, L.

Enter MARLOW, L.

MAR. What a bawling in every part of the house! I have scarce a moment's repose. If I go to the best room, there I find my host and his story. If I fly to the gallery, there we have my hostess with her courtesy down to the ground. I have at last got a moment to myself, and now for recollection. (*walks and muses.*)

MISS H. (*following him about*). Did you call, sir? did your honor call?

MAR. (*musing*). As for Miss Hardcastle, she's too grave and sentimental for me

MISS H. Did your honor call? (*she still places herself before him ; he turns away.*)

MAR. No, child. (*musing*) Besides, from the glimpse I had of her I think she squints.

MISS H. I am sure, sir, I heard the bell ring.

MAR. No, no. (*musing*) I have pleased my father, however, by coming down, and I'll to-morrow please myself by returning. (*taking out his tablets and perusing.*)

MISS H. Perhaps the other gentleman called, sir.

MAR. No, no, I tell you. (*looks full in her face*) Yes, child, I think I did call. I wanted—I wanted—I vow, child, you are vastly handsome.

MISS H. O. la, sir, you'll make one ashamed

MAR. Never saw a more sprightly, malicious eye. Yes, yes, my dear, I did call. Have you got any of your—a—what d'ye call it in the house?

MISS H. No, sir, we have been out of that these ten days.

MAR. One may call in this house, I find, to very little purpose. Suppose I should call for a taste, just by way of trial, of the nectar of your lips; perhaps I might be disappointed in that too.

MISS H. Nectar! nectar! that's a liquor there's no call for in these parts. French, I suppose. We keep no French wines here, sir.

Mar. Of true English growth, I assure you.

Miss H. Then it's odd I should not know it. We brew all sorts of wines in this house and I have lived here these eighteen years.

Mar. Eighteen years! Why, one would think, child, you kept the bar before you were born. How old are you?

Miss H. O, sir, I must not tell my age. They say women and music should never be dated.

Mar. To guess at this distance, you can't be much above forty. (*approaching*) Yet nearer. I don't think so much. (*approaching*) By coming close to some women they look younger still; but when we come very close indeed—(*attempting to kiss her.*)

Miss H. Pray, sir, keep your distance. One would think you wanted to know one's age as they do horses, by mark of mouth.

Mar. I protest, child; you use me extremely ill. If you keep me at this distance, how is it possible you and I can be ever acquainted?

Miss H. And who wants to be acquainted with you? I want no such acquaintance, not I. I'm sure you did not treat Miss Hardcastle in this obstropalous manner. I'll warrant me, before her you looked dashed, and kept bowing to the ground, and talked for all the world as if you was before a justice of the peace.

Mar. (*aside*). Egad! she has hit it, sure enough. (*to* Miss Hardcastle) In awe of her, child? Ha, ha, ha! A mere awkward, squinting thing; no, no! I find you don't know me. I laughed and rallied her a little; but I was unwilling to be too severe. No, I could not be too severe, curse me!

Miss H. Oh! then, sir, you are a favorite, I find among the ladies?

Mar. Yes, my dear, a great favorite; and yet hang me, I don't see what they find in me to follow. At the ladies' club in town, I am called their agreeable Rattle. Rattle, child, is not my real name, but one I'm known by. My name is Jenkins. Mr. Jenkins, my dear, at your service. (*offering to salute her.*)

Miss H. Hold, sir! you were introducing me to your club, not to yourself. And you're so great a favorite there, you say?

Mar. Yes, my dear. There's Mrs. Mantrap, Lady Betty Blackleg, the Countess of Cog, Mrs. Longhorns, old Miss Biddy Buckskin, and your humble servant, keep up the spirit of the place.

Miss H. Then it's a very merry place, I suppose?

Mar. Yes, as merry as cards, suppers, wine, and old women can make us.

Miss H. And their agreeable Rattle! Ha, ha, ha!

Mar. (*aside*). Egad! I don't quite like this chit. She looks knowing methinks. (*aloud*) You laugh, child!

Miss H. I can't but laugh, to think what time they all have for minding their work or their family.

Mar. (*aside*). All's well, she don't laugh at me. (*to* Miss Hardcastle) Do you ever work, child?

Miss H. Ay, sure. There's not a screen or quilt in the whole house but what can bear witness of that.

Mar. Odso! Then you must show me your embroidery. I embroider and draw patterns myself a little. If you want a judge of your work you must apply to me. (*seizing her hand.*)

Miss H. Ay, but the colors don't look well by candle-light. You shall see all in the morning. (*struggling.*)

Mar. And why not now, my angel? Pshaw! the landlord here? My good luck!   [*Exit*, L.

Enter Mr. Hardcastle, r., *who stands in surprise.**

Mr. H So, madam! so I find this is your modest lover. This is your humble admirer, that kept his eyes fixed on the ground, and only adored at humble distance. Kate, Kate, art thou not ashamed to deceive your father so?

Mis H. Never trust me, dear papa, but he's still the modest man I first took him for; you'll be convinced of it as well as I.

Mr. H By the hand of my body, I believe his impudence is infectious! Didn't I see him seize your hand! Didn't I see him haul you about like a milk-maid? and now you talk of his respect and his modesty, forsooth!

Miss H. But if I shortly convince you of his modesty, that he has only the faults that will pass off with time, and the virtues that will improve with age, I hope you'll forgive him.

Mr. H I tell you I'll not be convinced. I am convinced. He has scarcely been three hours in the house, and he has already encroached on all my prerogatives.

Miss H. S.r, I ask but this night to convince you.

Mr. H. You shall not have half the time, for I have thoughts of turning him out this very hour.

Miss H Give me that hour then, and I hope to satisfy you.

Mr H. Well, an hour let it be then. But I'll have no trifling with your father. All fair and open, do you mind me?

Miss H. I hope, sir, you have ever found that I considered your commands as my pride; for your kindness is such, that my duty as yet has been inclination?

[*Exeunt* Mr. Hardcastle *and* Miss Hardcastle, l.

CURTAIN.

———

ACT IV.

SCENE I.—*Same as Scene I., Act II.*

Enter Marlow, *followed by a* Servant, r.

Mar. I wonder what Hastings could mean by sending me so valuable a thing as a casket to keep for him, when he knows the only place I have is the seat of a post-coach at an inn door. Have you deposited the casket with the landlady, as I ordered you? Have you put it into her own hands?

Serv. (l.). Yes, your honor.

Mar. She said she'd keep it safe, did she?

Serv. Yes, she said she'd keep it safe enough; she asked me how I came by it? and she said she had a great mind to make me give an account of myself.   [*Exit* Servant, r.

Mar. (c.). Ha, ha, ha! They're safe, however. What an unaccountable set of beings have we got amongst! This little bar-maid though runs in my head most strangely, and drives out the absurdities of all the rest of the family; she's mine, she must be mine, or I'm greatly mistaken.

---

* The remainder of this Act was omitted at Wallack's Theatre.

HAST. (L.). Marlow here, and in spirits too!

MAR Give me joy, George! Crown me! shadow me with laurels!
Well, George, after all, we modest fellows don't want for success among
the women.

HAST. Some women, you mean. But what success has your honor's
modesty been crowned with now, that it grows so insolent upon us?

MAR. (C.). Didn't you see the tempting, brisk, lively little thing that
runs about the house with a bunch of keys to its girdle?

HAST. Well, and what then?

MAR. She's mine, you rogue, you! Such fire, such motion, such
eyes, such lips—but egad! she would not let me kiss them though.

HAST. But are you sure, so very sure of her?

MAR. Why, man, she talked of showing me her work above stairs,
and I'm to approve the pattern.

HAST. But how can you, Charles, go about to rob a woman of her
honor?

MAR. Pshaw! Pshaw! We all know the honor of the bar-maid of
an inn. I don't intend to rob her, take my word for it; there's nothing in the house I shan't honestly pay for.

HAST. I believe the girl has virtue.

MAR. And if she has, I should be the last man in the world that
would attempt to corrupt it.

HAST. You have taken care, I hope, of the casket I sent you to lock
up? Is it in safety?

MAR. Yes, yes. It's safe enough. I have taken care of it. But how
could you think the seat of a post-coach at an inn door a place of
safety? Ah, numskull! I have taken better precautions for you than
you did for yourself—I have——

HAST. What?

MAR. I have sent it to the landlady to keep for you.

HAST. To the landlady?

MAR. The landlady.

HAST. You did?

MAR. I did. She's to be answerable for its forthcoming, you know.

HAST. Yes, she'll bring it forth, with a witness.

MAR. Wasn't I right; I believe you'll allow that I acted prudently
upon this occasion?

HAST. (*aside*). He must not see my uneasiness.

MAR You seem a little disconcerted though, methinks. Sure nothing has happened?

HAST. No, nothing. Never was in better spirits in all my life. And
so you left it with the landlady, who, no doubt, very readily undertook
the charge?

MAR. Rather too readily. For she not only kept the casket, but
through her great precaution, was going to keep the messenger too.
(*laughing*) Ha, ha, ha!

HAST. (*laughing*). Ha, ha, ha! They're safe, however.

MAR. As a guinea in a miser's purse.

HAST. (*aside*). So now all hopes of fortune are at an end, and we
must set off without it. (*to* MARLOW) Well, Charles, I'll leave you to
your meditations on the pretty bar-maid, and— *laughing*) ha, ha, ha!
if you are as successful for yourself as you have been for me——

MAR. What then?

HAST. Why, then I wish you joy with all my heart

[*Exit* HASTINGS, L. MARLOW *sits in the background.*

Enter HARDCASTLE, L.

MR. H. I no longer know my own house. It's turned all topsy-turvy. His servants have got drunk already. I'll bear it no longer—and yet, from my respect for his father, I'll be calm. (*to* MARLOW) Mr. Marlow, your servant. (*bowing low*) I'm your very humble servant. (*takes a chair and sits.*)

MAR. Sir, your humble servant. (*aside*) What's to be the wonder now?

MR. H. I believe, sir, you must be sensible, sir, that no man alive ought to be more welcome than your father's son, sir? I hope you think so?

MAR. I do, from my soul, sir. I don't want much entreaty. I generally make my father's son welcome wherever he goes.

MR. H. (*rises*). I believe you do, from my soul, sir. But though I say nothing to your own conduct, that of your servants is insufferable. Their manner of drinking is setting a very bad example in this house, I assure you.

MAR. I protest, my very good sir, that's no fault of mine; if they don't drink as they ought they are to blame. I ordered them not to spare the cellar. I did. I assure you. (*calling off*, L.) Here, let one of my servants come up. (*to* HARDCASTLE) My positive directions were, that as I did not drink myself, they should make up for my deficiencies below.

MR. H. Then they have your orders for what they do! I'm satisfied!

MAR. They had, I assure you. You shall hear from one of themselves.

Enter SERVANT, *drunk*, L.

You, Jeremy, come forward, sirrah! what were my orders? Were you not told to drink freely, and call for what you thought fit, for the good of the house?

MR. H (*aside*). I begin to lose my patience.

SERV. (L.). Please your honor, liberty and Fleet Street for ever! Though I am but a servant. I'm as good as another man. I'll drink for no man before supper, sir. d—e! Good liquor will sit upon a good supper, but a good supper will not sit upon—hiccup—upon my conscience, sir.   [*Exit*, L.

MAR. (*rises and comes forward*). You see, my old friend, the fellow is as drunk as he possibly can be; I don't know what you'd have more, unless you'd have the poor devil soused in a beer-barrel.

MR. H. (*aside*). Zounds! He'll drive me distracted if I contain myself any longer. (*aloud*) Mr. Marlow, sir, I have submitted to your insolence for more than four hours, and I see no likelihood of its coming to an end. I'm now resolved to be master here, sir, and I desire that you and your drunken pack may leave my house directly.

MAR. Leave your house! Sure you jest, my good friend? What! when I'm doing what I can to please you?

MR. H. I tell you, sir, you don't please me; so I desire you'll leave my house.

MAR. (R. C.). Sure you cannot be serious? At this time of night, and such a night! You only mean to banter me?

MR. H. (R.). I tell you, sir, I am serious; and now that my passions are roused, I say this house is mine, sir, this house is mine, and I command you to leave it directly.

MAR. I shan't stir a step, I assure you. (*in a serious tone*) This your house. fellow? it's my house. This is my house. Mine while I choose to stay. What right have you to bid me leave this house, sir? I never met with such impudence, curse me, never in my whole life before.

MR. H. Nor I, confound me if ever I did. To come to my house to call for what he likes, to turn me out of my own chair, to insult the family, to order his servants to get drunk, and then to tell me " this house is mine, sir " By all that's impudent, it makes me laugh. Ha, ha, ha! Pray, sir, (*bantering*) as you take the house, what think you of taking the rest of the furniture? There's a pair of silver candlesticks, and there are a set of prints too. What think you of The Rake's Progress for your own apartment?

MAR. Bring me your bill, I say; and I'll leave you and your infernal house directly.

MR. H. Then there's a mahogany table, that you may see your face in.

MAR. My bill, I say.

MR. H. I had forgot the great chair, for your own particular slumbers, after a hearty meal.

MAR Zounds! bring me my bill, I say, and let's hear no more on't.

MR. H. Young man, young man, from your father's letter to me I was taught to expect a well-bred, modest man, as a visitor here, but now I find him no better than a coxcomb and a bully; but he will be down here presently, and shall hear more of it.   [*Exit.* L.

MAR How's this! Sure I've not mistaken the house? Everything looks like an inn. The servants cry, Coming; the attendance is awkward; the bar-maid too to attend us. But she's here, and will further inform me. Whither so fast, child? A word with you.

Enter MISS HARDCASTLE, L.

MISS H. Let it be short then. I'm in a hurry.

MAR. (c.). Pray, child, answer me one question. What are you, and what may your business in this house be?

MISS H. A relation of the family, sir.

MAR. What! A poor relation?

MISS H. Yes, sir. A poor relation appointed to keep the keys, and to see that the guests want nothing in my power to give them.

MAR. That is, you act as the bar-maid of this inn?

MISS H. Inn! O law! What brought that in your head? One of the best families in the country keep an inn! (*laughing*) Ha, ha, ha! old Mr. Hardcastle's house an inn!

MAR. Mr. Hardcastle's house! Is this house Mr. Hardcastle's house, child?

MISS H. Ay, sure. Whose else should it be?

MAR. So then all's out, and I have been d——y imposed on. O, confound my stupid head! I shall be laughed at over the whole town. I shall be stuck up in caricatures in all the print shops. The Dullissimo Maccaroni! To mistake this house of all others for an inn, and my father's old friend for an inn-keeper. What a swaggering puppy must he take me for! What a silly puppy do I find myself! There again, may I be hanged, my dear, but I mistook you for the bar-maid.

MISS H. Dear me! Dear me! I'm sure there's nothing in my behavior to put me upon a level with one of that stamp.

MAR. Nothing, my dear, nothing. But I was in for a list of blunders, and could not help making you a subscriber. My stupidity saw every thing the wrong way. I mistook your assiduity for assurance, and your simplicity for allurement. But it's over. This house I no more show my face in.

MISS H. I hope, sir, I have done nothing to disoblige you! I'm sure I should be sorry to affront any gentleman who has been so polite, and said so many civil things to me. I m sure I should be sorry —(*pretending to cry*) if he left the family upon my account. I'm sure I should be sorry people said anything amiss since I have no fortune but my character.

MAR (*aside*). By Heaven, she weeps! This is the first mark of tenderness I ever had from a modest woman, and it touches me

MISS H. But I m sure my family is as good as Miss Hardcastle's. and though I'm poor, that's no great misfortune to a contented mind, and until this moment I never thought it was bad to want fortune.

MAR. And why now, my pretty simplicity?

MISS H. Because it puts me at a distance from one, that if I had a thousand pound I would give it all to.

MAR. (*aside*). This simplicity bewitches me so that if I stay I'm undone. I must make one bold effort and leave her. (*aloud*) Your partiality in my favor, my dear, touches me most sensibly; and were I to live for myself alone, I could easily fix my choice. But to be plain with you, the difference of our birth, fortune, and education make an honorable connection impossible; and I can never harbor a thought of seducing simplicity, that trusted in my honor; or bringing ruin upon one whose only fault was being too lovely. [*Exit*, R.

MISS H. Generous man! I never knew half his merit till now. He shall not go if I have power or art to detain him. I'll still preserve the character in which I stooped to conquer, but will undeceive my papa, who, perhaps, may laugh him out of his resolution. [*Exit*, L.

Enter TONY *and* MISS NEVILLE, R.

TONY. Ay, you may steal for yourselves the next time; I have done my duty. She has got the jewels again, that's a sure thing; but she believes it was all a mistake of the servants.

MISS N. But my dear cousin, sure you won't forsake us in this distress? If she in the least suspects that I am going off, I shall certainly be locked up, or sent to my aunt Pedigree's, which is ten times worse.

TONY. To be sure, aunts of all kind are d—d bad things. But what can I do? I have got you a pair of horses that will fly like whistlejacket, and I'm sure you can't say but I have courted you nicely before her face. Here she comes, we must court a little more, for fear she should suspect us. (*they retire up, sit, and seem to fondle.*)

Enter MRS. HARDCASTLE, L.

MRS. H. (R.). Well, I was greatly fluttered, to be sure. But my son tells me it was all a mistake of the servants. I shan't be easy, however, till they are fairly married, and then let her keep her own fortune. (*sees them*) But what do I see! Fondling together, as I'm alive! I never saw Tony so sprightly before. Ah, have I caught you, my pretty doves! What billing, exchanging stolen glances, and broken murmurs, ah! (*they rise and come forward.*)

TONY. As for murmurs, mother, we grumble a little now and then to be sure. But there's no love lost between us.

Mrs. H. A mere sprinkling, Tony, upon the flame only to make it burn brighter.

Miss N. Cousin Tony promises to give us more of his company at home. Indeed, he shan't leave us any more. It won't leave us, cousin Tony, will it?

Tony. O, it's a pretty creature. No, I'd sooner leave my horse in a pond, than leave you when you smile upon one so. Your laugh makes you so becoming.

Miss N. Agreeable cousin! who can help admiring that natural humor, that pleasant, broad, red, thoughtless—(*patting his cheek*) Ah, it's a bold face.

Mrs. H. Pretty innocence!

Tony. I'm sure I always loved cousin Con's hazle eyes, and her pretty long fingers, that she twists this way and that over the haspicholls, like a parcel of bobbins.

Mrs. H. Ah, he would charm the bird from the tree. I never was so happy before. My boy takes after his father, poor Mr. Lumpkin, exactly. The jewels, my dear Con, shall be yours incontinently. You shall have them. Isn't he a sweet boy, my dear? You shall be married to-morrow, and we'll put off the rest of his education, like Dr. Drowsey's sermons, till a fitter opportunity.

Enter Diggory, r.

Dig. Where's the 'Squire? I have got a letter for your worship.

Tony. Give it to my mamma. She reads all my letters first.

Dig. I had orders to deliver it into your own hands.

Tony. Who does it come from?

Dig. Your worship mun ask that of the letter itself.   [*Exit*, r.

Tony. I could wish to know, though. (*turning the letter and gazing on it.*)

Miss N. (*aside*). Undone undone! A letter to him from Hastings. I know the hand. If my aunt sees it, we are ruined for ever. I'll keep her employed a little if I can. (*to* Mrs. Hardcastle) But I have not told you, madam, of my cousin's smart answer just now to Mr. Marlow. We so laughed. You must know, ma'am—this way a little, for he must not hear us. (*they sit and confer in the background*)

Tony (*in the c. of the fore-ground, still gazing*). A d—d cramp piece of penmanship as ever I saw in my life. I can read your print-hand very well. But here there are such handles, and shanks, and dashes, that one can scarce tell the head from tail. "To Anthony Lumpkin, Esq." It's very odd, I can read the outside of my letters, where my own name is, well enough; but when I come to open it, it's all—buzz. That's hard, very hard; for the inside of the letter is always the cream of the correspondence.

Mrs. H. (*laughing*). Ha, ha, ha! Very well, very well. And so my son was too hard for the philosopher?

Miss N. Yes, madam: but you must hear the rest, madam. A little more this way, or he may hear us. You'll hear how he puzzled him again.

Mrs. H. He seems strangely puzzled now himself, methinks.

Tony (*still gazing*). A d—d up-and-down hand, as if it was disguised in liquor. (*reading*) "Dear sir." Ay, that's that. Then there's an M, and a T, and an S, but whether the next be an izzard or an R, confound me, I cannot tell. (*they rise and come forward*)

Mrs. H. (r. c.). What's that, my dear? Can I give you any assistance?

Miss N. (*between them*). Pray, aunt, let me read it. Nobody reads a cramp hand better than I. (*twitching the letter from her*) Do you know who it is from ?

Tony. Can't tell, except from Dick Ginger, the feeder.

Miss N Ay, so it is. (*pretending to read*) " Dear Squire. Hoping that you're in health, as I am at this present. The gentlemen of the Shake-bag club has cut the gentlemen of the Goose-green quite out of feather. The odds—um—odd battle—um—long fighting—um.' Here, here! it's all about cocks, and fighting ; it's of no consequence—here, put it up, put it up. (*thrusting the crumpled letter upon him.*)

Tony. But I tell you, Miss, it's of all the consequence in the world. I would not lose the rest of it for a guinea! Here, mother, do you make it out. Of no·consequence ! (*giving* Mrs. Hardcastle *the letter*)

Mrs. H. How's this ? (*reads*) " Dear Squire, I am now waiting for Miss Neville, with a post-chaise and pair, at the bottom of the garden, but I find my horses yet unable to perform their journey. (Tony *goes to the background and sits*) I expect you'll assist us with a pair of fresh horses, as you promised. Dispatch is necessary, as the hag (ay, the hag), your mother, will otherwise suspect us. Yours. Hastings." Grant me patience ! I shall run distracted ! My rage chokes me !

Miss N. (c.) I hope, madam. you'll suspend your resentment for a few moments, and not impute to me any impertinence, or sinister design, that belongs to another.

Mrs. H. (*courtesying very low*, c.). Fine spoken, madam ; you are most miraculously polite and engaging, and quite the very pink of courtesy and circumspection, madam. (*turns to* Tony, *changing her tone*) And you, you great ill-fashioned oaf, with scarce sense enough to keep your mouth shut—were you too joined against me ? But I'll defeat all your plots in a moment. As for you, madam, since you have got a pair of fresh horses ready, it would be cruel to disappoint them. So, if you please, instead of running away with your spark. prepare, this very moment to run off with me. Your old aunt Pedigree will keep you secure, I'll warrant me. You too, sir. may mount your horse, and guard us upon the way. Here, Thomas, Roger, Diggory ! I'll show you that I wish you better than you do yourselves, 　　　[*Exit*, R.

Miss N. So, now I'm completely ruined.

Tony (*rises and advances*) Ay, that's a sure thing.

Miss N. What better could be expected from being connected with such a stupid fool, and after all the nods and signs I made him ?

Tony. By the laws, Miss, it was your own cleverness, and not my stupidity, that did your business. You were so nice and so busy with your Shake-bags, and Goose-greens, that I thought you could never be making believe.

Enter Hastings, R.

Hast. So, sir, I find by my servant, that you have shown my letter, and betrayed us. Was this well done, young gentleman ?

Tony. Here's another. Ask Miss there who betrayed you. Ecod ! it was her doing, not mine.

Enter Marlow, L.

Mar. So, I have been finely used here among you. Rendered contemptible, driven into ill-manners, despised, insulted, laughed at.

Tony. Here's another. We shall have old Bedlam broke loose presently.

Miss N. And there, sir, is the gentleman, to whom we all owe every obligation.

Mar. What can I say to him, a mere booby, an idiot, whose ignorance and age are a protection.

Hast. A poor contemptible booby, that would but disgrace correction.

Miss N. Yet with cunning and malice enough to make himself merry with all our embarrassments.

Hast. An insensible cub!

Mar. Replete with tricks and mischief.

Tony. Baw! d——e, but I'll fight you both one after the other—with baskets.

Mar. As for him, he's below resentment. But your conduct, Mr. Hastings, requires an explanation. You knew of my mistakes, yet would not undeceive me.

Hast. Tortured as I am with my own disappointments, is this a time for explanations? It is not friendly, Mr. Marlow.

Mar. But sir——

Miss N. Mr. Marlow, we never kept on your mistake till it was too late to undeceive you. Be pacified

Enter Diggory, l

Dig. My mistress desires you'll get ready immediately, madam. The horses are putting to. Your hat and things are in the next room. We are to go thirty mile before morning. [*Exit*, l.

Miss N. Well, well; I'll come presently. O, Mr. Marlow, if you knew what a scene of constraint and ill-nature lies before me, I'm sure it would convert your resentment into pity.

Mar. I m so distracted with a variety of passions that I don't know what I do. Forgive me, madam. George, forgive me. You know my hasty temper, and should not exasperate it.

Hast. The torture of my situation is my only excuse.

Miss N. Well, my dear Hastings, if you have that esteem for me that I think, that I am sure you have, your constancy for three years will but increase the happiness of our future connection. If——

Mrs. H. (*within*) Miss Neville, Constance! why, Constance, I say!

Miss N. I'm coming. Well, constancy. Remember, constancy is the word. [*Exit*, l.

Mar. (*to* Tony). You see now, young gentleman, the effects of your folly. What might be amusement to you is here disappointment, and even distress.

Tony (*from a reverie*). Ecod, I have hit it. It's here. Your hands. Yours, and yours, my poor Sulky. My boots there, ho! Meet me two hours hence at the bottom of the garden, and if you don't find Tony Lumpkin a more good-natured fellow than you thought for, I'll give you leave to take my best horse, and Bet Bouncer into the bargain.
[*Exeunt*, Tony *singing merrily*, r.

CURTAIN.

ACT V.

SCENE I.—*Same as Act II., Scene I.*

Enter SIR CHARLES MARLOW *and* MR. HARDCASTLE, R.

MR. H. (*laughing*). Ha, ha, ha! The peremptory tone in which he sent forth his sublime commands!

SIR CHARLES. And the reserve with which I suppose he treated all your advances!

MR. H. And yet he might have seen something in me above a common inn-keeper, too.

SIR C. Yes, Dick, but he mistook you for an uncommon inn-keeper, ha, ha, ha!

MR. H. Well, I'm in too good spirits to think of anything but joy. Yes, my dear friend, this union of our families will make our personal friendship hereditary; and though my daughter's fortune is but small——

SIR C. Why, Dick, will you talk of fortune to me? My son is possessed of more than a competence already, and can want nothing but a good and virtuous girl to share his happiness and increase it. If they like each other, as you say they do——

MR. H. If, man! I tell you they do like each other. My daughter as good as told me so.

SIR C. But girls are apt to flatter themselves, you know?

MR. H. I saw him grasp her hand in the warmest manner myself; and here he comes to put you out of your "ifs," I warrant you.

Enter MARLOW, L.

MAR. I come, sir, once more, to ask pardon for my strange conduct. I can scarce reflect on my insolence without confusion.

MR. H. Tut, boy, a trifle. You take it too gravely. An hour or two's laughing with my daughter will set all to rights again. She'll never like you the worse for it.

MAR. Sir, I shall be always proud of her approbation.

MR. H. Approbation is but a cold word, Mr. Marlow; if I am not deceived, you have something more than approbation thereabouts. You take me?

MAR. Really, sir, I have not that happiness.

MR. H. Come, boy, I'm an old fellow, and know what's what, as well as you that are younger. I know what has passed between you; but mum.

MAR. Sure, sir, nothing has passed between us but the most profound respect on my side, and the most distant reserve on hers. You don't think, sir, that my impudence has been passed upon all the rest of the family?

MR. H. Impudence! No, I don't say that. Not quite impudence. Though girls like to be played with, and rumpled too sometimes. But she has told no tales, I assure you.

MAR. May I die, sir, if I ever——

MR. H. I tell you, she don't dislike you; and as I'm sure you like her——

MAR. But why won't you hear me? By all that's just and true, I never gave Miss Hardcastle the slightest mark of my attachment, or

even the most distant hint to suspect me of affection. We had but one
interview, and that was formal, modest, and uninteresting.

MR. H. (*aside*). This fellow's formal, modest impudence is beyond
bearing.

SIR C. And you never grasped her hand, or made any protestations ?

MAR As Heaven is my witness, I came down in obedience to your
commands. I saw the lady without emotion, and parted without reluctance. I hope you'll exact no further proofs of my duty, nor prevent
me from leaving a house in which I suffer so many mortifications.

[*Exit*, L.

SIR C. I'm astonished at the air of sincerity with which he parted.

MR H. And I'm astonished at the deliberate intrepidity of his assurance.

SIR C. I dare pledge my life and honor upon his truth.

MR. H. Here comes my daughter, and I would stake my happiness
upon her veracity.

Enter MISS HARDCASTLE, R.

Kate, come hither, child. Answer us sincerely, and without reserve;
has Mr. Marlow made you any professions of love and affection ?

MISS H. The question is very abrupt, sir! But since you require
unreserved sincerity, I think he has.

MR H. (*to* SIR CHARLES). You see !

SIR C. And pray, madam, have you and my son had more than one
interview ?

MISS H. Yes, sir, several.

MR H. (*to* SIR CHARLES). You see !

SIR C. But did he profess any attachment ?

MISS H. A lasting one.

SIR C. Did he talk of love ?

MISS H. Much, sir !

SIR C. Amazing ! And all this formally ?

MISS H. Formally.

MR. H. Now, my friend, I hope you are satisfied.

SIR C. (L. C.). And how did he behave, madam ?

MISS H. (C). As most professed admirers do. Said some civil things
of my face, talked much of his want of merit, and the greatness of
mine; mentioned his heart, gave a short tragedy speech, and ended
with pretended rapture

SIR C. Now, I'm perfectly convinced, indeed. I know his conversation among women to be modest and submissive. This forward, cant-
ing, ranting manner by no means describes him, and I'm confident he
never sat for the picture.

MISS H. Then what, sir, if I should convince you to your face of my
sincerity.? If you and my papa, in about half an hour, will follow my
directions, you shall hear him declare his passion to me in person.

SIR C Agreed. And if I find him what you describe, all my happiness in him must have an end.

[*Exeunt* SIR CHARLES MARLOW. *and* MR. HARDCASTLE. R.

MISS H. And if you don't find him what I describe, I fear my happiness must never have a beginning.   [*Exit*, L.

SCENE II.—*Garden and small park in rear of* MR. HARDCASTLE'S
mansion. L. C. *and* L., *trees and ornamental shrubbery. On* R.
C. *and* 2 E , *a tree, looking rudely like a man with arm extended,
holding a pistol.*

Enter HASTINGS, L.

HAST. What an idiot am I, to wait here for a fellow who probably takes a delight in mortifying me? He never intended to be punctual, and I'll wait no longer. What do I see? It is he, and perhaps with news of my Constance!

Enter TONY, *booted and spattered with dirt,* R.

My honest 'Squire, I now find you a man of your word. This looks like friendship.

TONY. Ay, I'm your friend, and the best friend you have in the world, if you knew but all. This riding by night, by-the-bye, is cursedly tiresome. It has shook me worse than the basket of a stage-coach.

HAST. Well, but where have you left the ladies? I die with impatience.

TONY. Left them? Why, where should I leave them, but where I found them?

HAST. This is a riddle.

TONY. Riddle me this then. What's that goes round the house, and round the house, and never touches the house?

HAST. I'm still astray.

TONY. Why, that's it, mun I have led them astray. By jingo, there's not a pond or slough within five miles of the place but they can tell the taste of.

HAST. Ha, ha, ha! I understand; you took them in a round, while they supposed themselves going forward. And so you have at last brought them home again.

TONY. You shall hear. I first took them down Feather-bed-lane, where we stuck fast in the mud. I then rattled them crack over the stones of Up-and-down-Hill—I then introduced them to the gibbet on Crackskull Common, and from that, with a circumbendibus, I fairly lodged them in the horse-pond at the bottom of the garden.

HAST. But no accident, I hope?

TONY. No, no! only mother is confoundedly frightened. She thinks herself forty miles off. She's sick of the journey, and the cattle can scarce crawl. So if your own horses be ready, you may whip off with cousin, and I'll be bound that no soul here can budge an inch to follow you.

HAST. My dear friend, how can I be grateful?

TONY. Ay, now it's dear friend, noble 'Squire. Just now it was all idiot, cub, and run me through the body. D—n your way of fighting, I say. After we take a knock in this part of the country, we kiss and be friends. But if you had run me through the body, then I should be dead, and you might go kiss the hangman.

HAST. The rebuke is just. But I must hasten to relieve Miss Neville; if you keep the old lady employed, I promise to take care of the young one.   [*Exit,* R.

TONY. Never fear me. Here she comes. Vanish. She's got from the pond, and draggled up to the waist like a mermaid.

Enter MRS. HARDCASTLE, L. U. E   *Stage dark.*

MRS. H. O, Tony, I'm killed. Shook, battered to death. I shall never survive it. That last jolt has done my business.

TONY. Alack, mamma, it was all your own fault. You would be for running away by night, without knowing one inch of the way.

MRS. H. I wish we were at home again. I never met so many accidents in so short a journey. Drenched in the mud, overturned in a

ditch, stuck fast in a slcugh, jolted to a jelly, and at last to lose our
way. Whereabouts do you think we are. Tony?

Tony. By my guess, we should be upon Heavytree Heath, about
forty miles from home.

Mrs H. O lud! O lud! the most notorious spot in all the country.
We only want a robbery to make a complete night on't.

Tony. Don't be afraid, mamma, don't be afraid! two of the five that
kept here are hanged, and the other three may not find us. Don't be
afraid. Is that a man that's galloping behind us? No; it's only a
tree. Don't be afraid.

Mrs. H. The fright will certainly kill me.

Tony. Do you see anything like a black hat moving behind the
thicket?

Mrs. H. O, death!

Tony. No; it's only a cow. Don't be afraid, mother; don't be
afraid.

Mrs. H. As I'm alive, Tony, I see a man coming towards us. Ah!
I'm sure on't. If he perceives us, we are undone.

Tony (aside). Father-in-law, by all that's unlucky, come to take one
of his night walks. (to Mrs. Hardcastle) Ah, it's a highwayman, with
pistols as long as my arm. A d—d ill-looking fellow.

Mrs. H. Good Heaven defend us! He approaches!

Tony. Do you hide yourself in that thicket, and leave me to manage
him. If there be any danger, I'll cough and cry hem! When I cough
be sure to keep close. (Mrs. Hardcastle hides behind a tree, L. U. E.)

Enter Mr. Hardcastle, R.

Mr. H. I'm mistaken, or I heard voices of people in want of help.
Oh, Tony, is that you? I did not expect you so soon back. Are your
mother and her charge in safety?

Tony. Very safe, sir, at my aunt Pedigree's. Hem!

Mrs. H. (*from her retreat*). Ah, death; I find there's danger.

Mr. H. Forty miles in three hours! sure that's too much, my young-
ster.

Tony. Stout horses and willing minds make short journeys, as they
say. Hem!

Mrs. H. (*from behind the tree*). Sure he'll do the dear boy no
harm!

Mr. H. But I heard a voice here; I should be glad to know from
whence it came.

Tony. It was I, sir, talking to myself, sir. I was saying that forty
miles in three hours was very good going. Hem. As to be sure it
was. Hem! I have got a sort of cold by being out in the air. We'll
go in, if you please. Hem!

Mr. H. But if you talked to yourself, you did not answer yourself.
I am certain I heard two voices, and am resolved—(*raising his voice*)
to find the other out.

Mrs. H. (*running forward from behind*). O, lud! he'll murder my
poor boy, my darling. Here, good gentleman, whet your rage upon
me. Take my money, life, but spare that young gentleman, spare my
child, if you have any mercy!

Mr. H. My wife, as I am a Christian! From whence can she come,
or what does she mean?

Mrs. H. (*kneeling*). Take compassion on us, good Mr. Highwayman!
Take our money, our watches, all we have, but spare our lives. We

will never bring you to justice, indeed we won't, good Mr. Highwayman!

Mr. H. I believe the woman's out of her senses. What, Dorothy, don't you know me?

Mrs. H. Mr. Hardcastle, as I live! My fears blinded me. But who, my dear, could have expected to meet you here, in this frightful place, so far from home? What has brought you to follow us?

Mr. H. Sure, Dorothy, you have not lost your wits? So far from home, when you are within forty yards of your own door. (*to* Tony) This is one of your old tricks, you graceless rogue, you. (*to* Mrs. Hardcastle) Don't you know the gate, and the mulberrytree; and don't you remember the horsepond, my dear?

Mrs. H. Yes, I shall remember the horsepond as long as I live; I have caught my death in it. (*to* Tony) And is it to you, you graceless varlet, I owe all this? I'll teach you to abuse your mother, I will.

Tony. Ecod! mother, all the parish says you have spoiled me, and so you may take the fruits on't.

Mrs. H. (*following*). I'll spoil you, I will.   [*Exeunt*, R.

SCENE III.—*Same as Act I., Scene I.*

Enter Sir Charles Marlow *and* Miss Hardcastle, L.

Sir C. What a situation am I in? If what you say appears, I shall then find a guilty son. If what he says be true, I shall then lose one that, of all others, I most wished for a daughter.

Miss H. I am proud of your approbation, and to show I merit it, if you will conceal yourselves behind that screen, you shall hear his ex-. plicit declaration. But he comes.

Sir C. I'll to your father, and keep him to the appointment.
                              [*Exit* Sir Charles, L. C.
Enter Marlow, L.

Mar. (L.). Though prepared for setting out, I come once more to take leave; nor did I till this moment know the pain I feel in the separation.

Miss H. (*in her own manner*). I believe these sufferings cannot be very great, sir, which you can so easily remove. A day or two longer perhaps might lessen your uneasiness, by showing the little value of what you think proper to regret.

Mar. (*aside*, L. C.). This girl every moment improves upon me. (*aloud*) It must not be, madam. I have already trifled too long with my heart. My very pride begins to submit to my passion; and nothing can restore me to myself but this painful effort of resolution.

Miss H. (C.). Then go, sir. I'll urge nothing more to detain you. Though my family be as good as her's you come down to visit, and my education, I hope, not inferior, what are these advantages without equal affluence? I must remain contented with the slight approbation of imputed merit; I must have only the mockery of your addresses, while all your serious aims are fixed on fortune.

Enter Mr. Hardcastle *and* Sir Charles Marlow, D. C., *and remain unseen by* Marlow.

Mar. By Heavens, madam, fortune was ever my smallest consideration. Your beauty at first caught my eye; for who could see that without emotion? But every moment that I converse with you steals in some new grace, heightens the picture and gives it stronger expression. What at first seemed rustic plainness, now appears refined simplicity. What seemed forward assurance, now strikes me as the result of courageous innocence and conscious virtue—I am now determined to say, madam, and I have too good an opinion of my father's discernment, when he sees you, to doubt his approbation.

Miss H No Mr. Marlow; I will not, cannot detain you. Do you think I could suffer a connection in which there is the smallest room for repentance? Do you think I would take the mean advantage of a transient passion, to load you with confusion? Do you think I could ever relish that happiness which was acquired by lessening yours? Do you think I could ever catch at the confident addresses of a secure admirer?

Mar. (*kneeling*). Does this look like security? Does this look like confidence? No, madam, every moment that shows me your merit, only serves to increase my diffidence and confusion. Here let me continue——

Sir C. I can hold it no longer. (*advancing*) Charles, Charles, how hast thou deceived me! Is this your indifference, your uninteresting conversation?

Mr. H Your cold contempt, your formal interview? What have you to say now?

Mar. That I'm all amazement! What can it mean?

Mr. H. It means that you can say and unsay things at pleasure; that you can address a lady in private, and deny it in public; that you have one story for us, and another for my daughter.

Mar. Daughter! this lady your daughter.

Mr. H. Yes, sir, my only daughter. My Kate; whose else should she be?

Mar. O, the devil!

Miss. H Yes, sir, that very identical tall, squinting lady, you were pleased to take me for. (*courtseying*) She that you addressed as the mild, modest, sentimental man of gravity, and the bold, forward, agreeable Rattle of the ladies' club; (*laughing*) ha, ha, ha!

Mar. Zounds! there's no bearing this; it's worse than death!

Miss H. In which of your characters, sir, will you give us leave to address you? As the faltering gentleman, with looks on the ground that speaks just to be heard, and hates hypocrisy; or the loud, confident creature, that keeps it up with Mrs. Mantrap, and old Mrs. Biddy Buckskin till three in the morning? Ha, ha, ha!

Mar. O, curse on my noisy head! I never attemped to be impudent yet that I was not taken down. I must be gone!

Mr. H. By the hand of my body, but you shall not. I see it was all a mistake, and I rejoice to find it. You shall not, sir, I tell you. I know she'll forgive you. Won't you forgive him, Kate? We'll all forgive you Take courage, man. (*they retire*, Miss Hardcastle tormenting Marlow.)

Enter Mrs. Hardcastle *and* Tony, R.

Mrs. H. So, so, they're gone off. Let them go, I care not.

Mr. H. Who gone?

Mrs H. My dutiful niece and her gentleman, Mr. Hastings, from town. He who came down with our modest visitor here.

Sir C. Who, my honest George Hastings? As worthy a fellow as lives, and the girl could not have made a more prudent choice.

Enter HAS·INGS *and* MISS NEVILLE, L.

MRS. H. (*aside*). What, returned so soon? I begin not to like it.

HAST. (*to* HARDCASTLE). For my late attempt to fly off with your niece, let my present confusion be my punishment. We are now come back, to appeal from your justice to your humanity. By her father's consent I first paid her my addresses, and our passions were first founded on duty.

MR. H. I'm glad they are come back to reclaim their due. Come, hither, Tony, boy. Do you refuse this lady's hand whom I now offer you?

TONY. What signifies my refusing? You know I can't refuse her till I'm of age, father!

MR. H. While I thought concealing your age, boy, was likely to conduce to your improvement, I concurred with your mother's desire to keep it secret; but since I find she turns it to a wrong use, I must now declare you have been of age these three months.

TONY. Of age! Am I of age, father?

MR. H. Above three months.

TONY. Then you'll see the first use I'll make of my liberty. (*taking* MISS NEVILLE's *hand*) Witness all men by these presents, that I, Anthony Lumpkin, Esquire, of Blank place, refuse you, Constantia Neville, spinster, of no place at all, for my true and lawful wife. So Constantia Neville may marry whom she pleases, and Tony Lumpkin is his own man again.   [*Exit*, L.

SIR C. O, brave 'Squire!

HAST. My worthy friend!

MRS. H. My dutiful offspring!

MAR. Joy, my dear George, I give you joy sincerely. And could I prevail upon my little tyrant here to be less arbitrary, I should be the happiest man alive, if you would return me the favor.

HAST. (*to* MISS HARDCASTLE). Come, madam, you are now driven to the very last scene of all your contrivances. I know you like him, I'm sure he loves you; and you must and shall have him.

MR. H. (*joining their hands*). And I say so too. And, Mr. Marlow, if she makes as good a wife as she has a daughter, I don't believe you'll ever repent your bargain. So, boy, take her; and as you have been mistaken in the mistress, my wish is, that you may never be mistaken in the wife.

CURTAIN.

TONY LUMPKIN'S SONG IN "SHE STOOPS TO CONQUER."*

---

* For the words see page 15.

Let school - mas - ters puz - zle their brain With

grammar, and nonsense, and learn-ing, Good li - quor, I

stout - ly main - tain, Gives ge - nius a bet - ter dis -

- cern-ing. Let them brag of their hea-then-ish gods, Their

Le - thes, their Styx - es, and Stygians, Their quis, and their

quæs, and their quods! They're all but a par - cel of Pi-geons!

To - rod-dle, to - rod-dle, to - roll! To - rod-dle, to - rod-dle, to - rod-dle, to - rod-dle, to - rod-dle, to - roll! Here's a health to the Three Jol - ly Pi-geons!

D. C.

www.ingramcontent.com/pod-product-compliance
Lightning Source LLC
Chambersburg PA
CBHW032117080426
42733CB00008B/973